MW01505014

The beauty of Haber's book is its focus on the phenomenology of the therapeutic relationship, illuminating the dialectic of developmental yearnings and defensive retreats from individuality as played out in the experiences of both patient and analyst.

Robert D. Stolorow is founding and senior member of the Institute of Contemporary Psychoanalysis, Los Angeles

Darren Haber's outstanding study of addictive worlds interweaves contemporary psychoanalytic perspectives with rich existential metaphors found in the works of Camus, Beckett, Kafka and others. The psychotherapy of addiction, so fraught with histories of trauma and all manner of antidotal curative fantasies, opens up under his insightful gaze as never before.

George Atwood is corresponding member of the Institute of Contemporary Psychoanalysis, Los Angeles

In his provocative and contemporary work, Haber commands cutting edge psychoanalytic thought in pointing us toward a more compassionate, phenomenologically based, and rigorously contextualized understanding of addiction and its treatment. His rendering of the problem of disavowed aspects of selfhood, and its concomitant evasion of living an authentically affect-laden life, offers a much-needed corrective to the more familiar and traditional modes of organizing and pathologizing addictive/compulsive processes. Personal, astute, and moving, Haber's work is a must-read for clinicians and patients alike.

William J. Coburn is a member of the Institute of Contemporary Psychoanalysis in Los Angeles, and Founding Editor Emeritus of Psychoanalysis, Self & Context

Addiction, Accommodation, and Vulnerability in Psychoanalysis

This book explores the compulsions and trauma that underlie addiction, using an intersubjective approach in seeking to understand the inspirations and challenges arising from the psychoanalytic treatment of addiction, compulsivity, and related dissociative conditions.

Drawing on insights from his own analytic practice and personal experience, in addition to the work of Stolorow, Brandchaft and Winnicott, among others, Haber considers the complex ways in which addiction becomes woven into a person's life, and analyses how it interacts with other problems such as depression and anxiety, self-fragmentation, and ambivalence about treatment. Haber creatively integrates the work of Camus, Kafka, and Beckett to further contemplate the dilemmas that can arise during the clinical process and, in identifying his own and his patients' vulnerabilities and contradictions, provides an honest, humorous and sometimes painful account of what happens in the consulting room.

With its use of rich clinical material and an accessible and vivid writing style, this book will appeal to all psychoanalysts and psychotherapists working with patients affected by addiction, as well as other professionals seeking new insights into effective strategies for treating this most challenging malady.

Darren M. Haber, PsyD, MFT, is a psychoanalyst in Los Angeles. He has published online at the LA Review of Books, Psyche.co, and the APA blog. He frequently appears in the journal *Psychoanalysis, Self and Context*. He blogs regularly at GoodTherapy.org, Psychology Today and other sites. His website is www.therapistinlosangeles.com.

Relational Perspectives Book Series

ADRIENNE HARRIS,
STEVEN KUCHUCK & EYAL ROZMARIN
Series Editors

STEPHEN MITCHELL
Founding Editor

LEWIS ARON
Editor Emeritus

The Relational Perspectives Book Series (RPBS) publishes books that grow out of or contribute to the relational tradition in contemporary psychoanalysis. The term relational psychoanalysis was first used by Greenberg and Mitchell to bridge the traditions of interpersonal relations, as developed within interpersonal psychoanalysis and object relations, as developed within contemporary British theory. But, under the seminal work of the late Stephen A. Mitchell, the term relational psychoanalysis grew and began to accrue to itself many other influences and developments. Various tributaries—interpersonal psychoanalysis, object relations theory, self psychology, empirical infancy research, feminism, queer theory, sociocultural studies and elements of contemporary Freudian and Kleinian thought—flow into this tradition, which understands relational configurations between self and others, both real and fantasied, as the primary subject of psychoanalytic investigation.

We refer to the relational tradition, rather than to a relational school, to highlight that we are identifying a trend, a tendency within contemporary psychoanalysis, not a more formally organized or coherent school or system of beliefs. Our use of the term relational signifies a dimension of theory and practice that has become salient across the wide spectrum of contemporary psychoanalysis. Now under the editorial supervision of Adrienne Harris, Steven Kuchuck and Eyal Rozmarin, the Relational Perspectives Book Series originated in 1990 under the editorial eye of the late Stephen A. Mitchell. Mitchell was the most prolific and influential of the originators of the relational tradition. Committed to dialogue among psychoanalysts, he abhorred the authoritarianism that dictated adherence to a rigid set of beliefs or technical restrictions. He championed open discussion, comparative and integrative approaches, and promoted new voices across the generations. Mitchell was later joined by the late Lewis Aron, also a visionary and influential writer, teacher and leading thinker in relational psychoanalysis.

Included in the Relational Perspectives Book Series are authors and works that come from within the relational tradition, those that extend and develop that tradition, and works that critique relational approaches or compare and contrast them with alternative points of view. The series includes our most distinguished senior psychoanalysts, along with younger contributors who bring fresh vision. Our aim is to enable a deepening of relational thinking while reaching across disciplinary and social boundaries in order to foster an inclusive and international literature.

A full list of titles in this series is available at https://www.routledge.com/Relational-Perspectives-Book-Series/book-series/LEARPBS.

Addiction, Accommodation, and Vulnerability in Psychoanalysis

Circles Without a Center

Darren M. Haber

Routledge
Taylor & Francis Group

LONDON AND NEW YORK

Cover image: PublicDomainPictures / 17902 images; Pixabay.com

First published 2023
by Routledge
4 Park Square, Milton Park, Abingdon, Oxon OX14 4RN

and by Routledge
605 Third Avenue, New York, NY 10158

Routledge is an imprint of the Taylor & Francis Group, an informa business

© 2023 Darren M. Haber

British Library Cataloguing in Publication Data
A catalogue record for this book is available from the British Library

Library of Congress Cataloging-in-Publication Data
A catalog record has been requested for this book

ISBN: 9781032210100 (hbk)
ISBN: 9781032210117 (pbk)
ISBN: 9781003266358 (ebk)

DOI: 10.4324/9781003266358

Typeset in Times New Roman
by Taylor & Francis Books

I devote this book to the blessed memory of my sister, Andrea L. Haber.

Contents

Credits List

Introduction

Hello and welcome. This volume represents my earliest efforts at writing about the inspirations and challenges of psychoanalysis (or analytic psychotherapy), especially in regard to treating addiction. Analytic writing on this topic is often categorized as a specialty or niche onto itself; some will say they don't "'do' addiction.' Such segregation is ironic, given addiction's sociocultural prevalence, the shadow of our technophilic materialism. Compulsive processes occur of course on a complicated spectrum, in a variety of antidotal mitigations, be it booze or pot or Netflix or work, often averting traumatic affect that has yet to be named let alone recognized, yet omnisciently pervasive.

Addictive processes and their treatment are much of the time an existential grind, with an amplification of psychic vulnerability and habitual resistance to same, with hints of tragicomic absurdities in patients' lives and treatments. Thus my attempts to theoretically integrate Camus, Kafka, and Beckett. These authors have made a profound impact, resonating currently in my immersion in intersubjective-systems theory (also known as phenomenological contextualism), itself deeply influenced by the work of Heidegger, Gadamer, Levinas, Buber, Wittgenstein, and others.

It can be challenging to co-determine with patients *what* is an addiction and what is not, a question highly subjectivized and often contentious. Determining the social acceptability of drinking or drug use also involves complex sociocultural factors and patient histories, including fraught experiences of race, gender, neurodivergence, and so on.

Addiction is complicated, given the relational knottedness of addictive systems, never more so than with patients whose partners, parents, or children are wrestling with addiction, which the patient anxiously hopes to ameliorate. At times in such treatment, it is the loved one's subjectivity and not the patient's which is rigidly foregrounded. 'How can I get them to stop?' is a question I hear almost every day. 'Who are we talking about?' is often the answer, privately or implicitly.

Such complexity, the confusing swirl of minds and perspectives amidst chaos—combined with incongruent inflexibility—sooner or later grips the *dyad,* often haunting to the atmosphere. This is of chief interest to me here,

DOI: 10.4324/9781003266358-1

and why literature is so helpful in giving poetic or metaphorical form to apparently intractable dilemmas. Addiction in the end is an all-too-human problem, tangled and dense.

What I chiefly emphasize is the affective or systemic functioning of compulsivity. Patients intensely attached to video games or social media, for instance, find habitual, dissociative numbing *and* vast potential for connection unavailable elsewhere, especially during a pandemic. (All the chapters here, save the last, were written and edited before the pandemic and the sociocultural tumult that followed, including the emergence of the social justice movement.)

I find literature helpful to analytic processes, a counterbalance in an age of evidence or 'data,' as with neuroscience and its semi-magical allure. Such hard-wired information, however fascinating or useful, tends also to reinforce the illusion of individualism, an intrapsychic path to monadic emancipation, decontextualizing the very relational patterns of abuse or neglect which in patients' histories have been so neglected.

Scientism can augment but not replace relational complexity. Patients may understand *how* their brain works differently, but not the existential implication for instance of an unrecognized abandonment leading to the ameliorations of drugs, alcohol, sex, and so on. The danger is not the data but what we make of it, a sometimes-illusory temptation for cognition to purge systemically 'unacceptable' affect once and for all.

Compulsivities, along these lines, often serve as hidden regulators of disordered systems or contexts, as with, for instance, unacknowledged demands for accommodating those in authority. Chapters 7 and 8 examine how compulsive soothing becomes for patients a coping against the agonies of caregiver abandonment, accommodation, or invasiveness, historically and in current (co)transferences—all stubbornly unseen.

I hope to illustrate throughout how relationally-minded analysts are in a good position to understand relational mitigation, on the heels of relational trauma—with adjunct support if needed via 12-step or other groups, consultation with addiction specialists, referrals to outpatient programs, and so on. My hope is the bridging of these often-disparate theoretical worlds, with a deeply attuned exploration and understanding of patients' subjectivities at the center of the work.

Any analytic treatment involves trial and error, and I would encourage interested analysts, as with patients, to embrace clinical flexibility, ignore pressure to find *the* correct path where addiction is concerned. Our willingness to look into options for adjunct support groups, of patients' experimenting with harm reduction (versus total abstinence), of educating ourselves in service to patients' well-being, is all to the good, providing flexibility for often rigid self-organizations. An attitude of our needing help to help patients, can be useful, contagious, and even necessary, and not just in regard to addiction alone, depending as always on specifics.

It also needs to be said that some courses of treatment (including analysis) are more privileged or accessible than others. I have clinically observed unmistakable differences between my position and those of some of my patients, in terms of class, race, and gender (among other things). Again not a simple matter, with commonality also found among those recovering from addiction or addictive systems, with patients from a broad spectrum of backgrounds.

Though not broad enough, I fear. I hope to explore and expand upon such themes in future work.

Finally, I wish to thank some of those who have supported me along the way, including Penelope Starr-Karlin, George Atwood, Bob Stolorow, Peter Maduro, Junie Mayes, Margaret Allan, Gordon Berger, Abby Vinson, Daniel Goldin, Mark Winitsky, Bill Coburn, Bradley Jones, Marcia Dobson, Suzi Naiburg, Diana Lidofsky, Sarah Mendelsohn, Harry Paul, and others too numerous to name. Thank you to Kate Hawes, Georgina Clutterbuck, and Hannah Wright for shepherding me through this process. I also thank my wife and daughter, Elaine and Lucy Haber, for their ceaseless backing.

Chapter 1

Yearning for Godot

Repetition and Vulnerability in Psychoanalysis

ESTRAGON: I am happy.
VLADIMIR: We are happy....
ESTRAGON: What do we do, now that we are happy?
VLADIMIR: Wait for Godot.

Estragon groans. Silence.

(Beckett, 1954, p. 39)

Lately it seems to me that, within the psychoanalytic process, both patient and analyst find themselves, sooner or later, waiting for Godot.

The patient, especially when new to analysis or analytic therapy, comes with a long-held hope of transcending existential pain and struggle. This hope often, especially with patients struggling with addiction (the majority of my caseload), takes a literal or concretized form. Here a patient awaits a romantic partner or some *actual* caregiver-figure, possibly including the therapist, to literally transform or 'rescue' them from misery, in a way that *guarantees* ongoing care and attunement, and detours around unspeakable or unnamable (Atwood, 2012) traumatic feeling-states which 'return one again and again to an [earlier] experience of traumatization ... fracturing one's sense of unitary selfhood' (Stolorow, 2015, p. 133).

We analysts recognize that such concretized yearnings on the part of the patient, for the reliable circumvention of such overwhelming states, might represent a curative fantasy (Orenstein, 1995)—implying the eventual disillusionment of a patient's hopes when such fantasy fails to materialize. For some analysts, for reasons I shall explicate, this may lead to a dread or apprehension of 'failing' or harming the patient, which in turn may foster repetitions, enactments or ritualizations within the dyad.

We understand, intellectually at least, that if any actual self-expansiveness is to be found, it will likely involve the revisiting of the dreaded, painful affect which a patient has repetitively numbed or averted since an archaic environment demanded it. In fact, the need to repetitively numb such affect is often what fuels addiction in the first place.

DOI: 10.4324/9781003266358-2

It is easy to underestimate the potent persistence of an archaic 'command' to maintain the sequestering of trauma-related affect. Such an affective amputation continues to trap the patient in the remains of a structural tie, to caregivers who initially demanded the blunting or segregation of 'entire zones of [the patient's] subjectivity' (Brandchaft, 2010, p. 199). With many if not most of my patients, some form of pathological accommodation is at issue, an underlying adhesion to archaic demands for affective riddance.

Brandchaft often noted how such rigid self-organizations sustain a terror of change, *no matter how deeply such change is desired by the patient.* An irreconcilable paradox: Godot is wanted or desperately needed, while such need *itself* must remain 'offstage'—forbidden, a sign of shameful weakness. This can then lead to a seeking of *concretized* solutions, bypassing vulnerability.

Of course, it is that very vulnerability which may be the 'Godot' we analysts seek, awaiting the emergence of painful or shameful affect, for the sake of empathic inquiry and relational home-building (Stolorow, 2007). How or how long to sustain such inquiry remains an ongoing question, as we hope to cultivate an increased tolerance of a patient's vulnerability, existential 'permission' for fundamental differentiation while ensuring that current *analytic* ties remain intact. Some patients decide that this is too risky or 'slow,' and would rather work with a life-coach, fitness trainer, or psychic reader. Many patients become dismayed at 'how long this takes,' in a marketplace glutted with 'quick fixes.'

Part of the challenge for patients trapped in rigidly accommodative self-organizations, is the struggle to *safely* exit 'what has become a closed and noxious system' (Brandchaft, 1994, p. 63); such an exit is perceived, then and now, as stepping off an existential cliff. Thus, the patient waits for a Godot who *guarantees* freedom while preserving cohesion and aversion of a feared breakdown (Winnicott, 1974). An analyst's fear of the latter can lead to the provision of antidotal (Stolorow, Atwood & Orange, 1997) reassurances, affective detours.

Of course, some degree of 'antidote' may be necessary, as the challenge with many such patients is that *emotionality itself*—especially including developmental desires—remains 'a solitary and unacceptable state, a sign of loathsome defect ... that must be eliminated' (Stolorow & Stolorow, 1987, p. 72). This can mean that—depending on the acuity of a patient's trauma, and self-protectiveness—a patient's 'Godot' is deemed ready to arrive *when and only when* an analyst has enabled them to bury 'verboten' aspects of selfhood six feet under. Brandchaft (1994), ever prescient, observed that such 'insidious defensive processes' ensure that 'development on the basis of authenticity of experience ... is repetitively foreclosed' (pp. 62–63).

I am beginning to understand how impossibly paradoxical are such developmental yearnings, for patients seeking relief from terrifying affect which *has not and cannot even be acknowledged* intersubjectively. This in turn only underscores the furtive seeking of concretized or ritualized means of relief, which protect even as they foreclose authentic strivings. (Addictive behaviors, for instance, both fleetingly 'satisfy' and exacerbate desires for relational expansiveness.)

Often a patient's emotionality has been so devalued that its toxicity is beyond question, simply how things are, an 'absolutized belief' (Brandchaft, 2010, p. 199), no matter what intellectualized lip service is given to 'feelings;' vulnerable or vitalizing self-expression, seeking a more intimate relatedness, remains 'an inarguable demonstration of ... stupidity and willfulness' (Brandchaft, 1994, p. 63).

Nothing to be done, as Estragon says in *Godot*.

Often a patient's hopes for signs of analytic 'progress,' guardrails against a terrifying plunge, imply the elimination of the analyst's own uncertainties and limitations, what Stolorow (2007) calls 'finitude'—our human imperfections, or being-with-uncertainty, an inability to foreclose a patient's existential suffering or portkeys perceived as potentially fatal. As we shall see, the latter is no exaggeration, given some patients' archaically unrecognized trauma. 'It feels like it will never end,' some patients say after experiencing retraumatization, as the recurrence of such long-unacknowledged pain appears to attack their very going-on-being (Winnicott, 1965). Uncertainty is itself traumatic for many patients (Brothers, 2008)—and an inevitable aspect of the analytic process.

In the meantime, dyadic glimpses of the very spirit which the analyst hopes to free are precisely what may frighten a patient into self-protective paralysis or retreat. Such self-protections are usually followed, in my experience, by a collapse into shame and self-loathing, as the patient feels he is disappointing a caregiver-figure yet again. Or we might sense implicit or overt demands that analysis 'get somewhere,' especially when a patient has been pushed into therapy by a partner or family member demanding 'progress.' We may become disappointed in *ourselves* if we sense we are disappointing the patient in this instance.

The patient might, in other words, begin to resemble Beckett's Pozzo or Lucky, 'Godot's' master and servant, respectively—helpless or demanding in the extreme—rather than the sibling-in-darkness, or co-dweller within the relational home (Stolorow, 2007) we hope to provide.

We analysts are thus ourselves waiting: for signs of our own effectiveness, confirmation that patients understand, or recognize, in some part at least, our care or concern for them.

We may also be waiting for signs of enlivening relatedness, the fleeting appearance or exploration of developmental strivings, for emotionality to become valued rather than loathed; for opportunities to employ 'spontaneous disciplined engagement' (Lichtenberg, 1999)—for some clues, so help us, that all this effort is 'getting somewhere.' Repetition can be wearying, such as a patient's epically-embedded ritualizations or self-protections, or other manifestations of an 'exacerbated [transference] dilemma,' which puts the analyst in the grip 'of a requirement to provide the patient with an unbroken ... experience uncontaminated by painful repetitions of past childhood traumata' (Stolorow, 1993, p. 33), forestalling analytic traction.

Examples of such 'grips' include, in my case, a patient's seeking a 'prescription' of how to stop 'wanting' to drink or use drugs (often to please an impatient other); determining whether or not he has a frightful disease based on somaticized symptoms; or how to exit an abusive relationship in a way that ensures *the other* will not collapse. In such cases, a patient often becomes frustrated or deflated if I cannot detect or articulate their feelings from afar, *conceptually* perceived, that I am 'forcing' them to dwell in pain rather than analyze or surgically remove such affect for the sake of 'curing' or cleansing them, finally, of overwhelming, obtrusive, or even contemptible emotion.

Here too I may sense I am 'failing' the patient in my inability to provide an assuredly safe prescription, as if my own analytic orientation, or fallible subjectivity (Orange, 2006) is shamefully at issue, that if I come up short or offer something 'deficient,' the patient may become endangered, or exit—as they sometimes do.

ESTRAGON: Use your intelligence, can't you?

Vladimir uses his intelligence.

VLADIMIR: I remain in the dark.

(p. 12)

Such situations—the Godot situation generally, with these specific variations—can be especially problematic for those of us who survived a 'gifted child' (Miller, 1997) upbringing, resulting in a fraught intersubjective resonance (Stolorow & Atwood, 2016) when vulnerability becomes perceived, by patient and/or analyst, as dangerously or contemptuously risky. An eerie *déjà vu* ensues, as I once again appear required to provide an asymmetrically 'perfect' responsiveness—lest I become a kind of 'anti-Godot' to a person I hope to help. In my own childhood, not knowing or having answers to 'obvious' questions asked by agitated or angry caregivers—in an attempt to prove that the feelings I was expressing were 'immature' or 'irrational'—marked me as inadequate, a longstanding killer-organizing principle (Stolorow, 1999) of my own.

Atwood (2015) describes this 'gifted child' scenario as being a 'traumatic condition' called 'the situation of the lost childhood,' which 'has developed early in the lives of almost every psychotherapist I have known,' especially those of us who treat acutely disordered or dissociated patients. In such histories, whenever the child or 'little psychotherapist' dares to pursue vitalizing self-expression, 'the parental response may be, "Why are you killing me?"' (all quotes, p. 150).

Atwood describes how such a child becomes beholden to the needs of parents for whom differentiation produces 'reactions of great distress ... sometimes rage' (p. 150). Such a child may later, as an analyst, fear 'killing' a patient by disappointing her in not 'satisfying' subtly or overtly concretized pursuits. Thus, instead of becoming a kind of Godot for patients, we find ourselves turning into Godot's *assassin,* threatening a patient's initial hopes and, possibly, their ongoing participation (prompting an urgent visit to the psychic reader).

Yet eventually we do, of course, step on toes, by misinterpreting or becoming misattuned at a crucial moment, in a way reminiscent of a patient's wounding caregivers—landing us in the Ferenczian (1932) hot water of an analyst symbolically (or *literally,* for some patients) repeating 'with his own hands the act of murder previously perpetuated against the patient. In contrast to the original murderer, however, he is not allowed to deny his guilt' (p. 58).

Intellectually we know such murder is symbolic, transferential. But experientially (Coburn, 2002), in the analytic 'trenches,' it is not so simple. Consider what transpired between a patient and a colleague of mine—a well-respected, seasoned analyst—nine months or so into treatment. His middle-aged patient, a survivor of extreme childhood neglect and abandonment, had since the beginning vacillated between trusting and not trusting the analyst; she had been callously abandoned over and over again by her caregivers, a torturous repetition never acknowledged, now appearing in the analysis as a persistent ambivalence. Her older brother was deeply narcissistic, chronically ill and drug-addicted; she grew used to the notion that what little attunement she received amidst volatility would prove fleeting, quickly withdrawn, linking her yearnings with the apprehension of traumatic pain.

My colleague awaited signs of traction and trust, as she continued to oscillate: hypervigilant she was, like many abandoned patients. Eventually a vulnerable yearning stirred: a quiet hope, tentatively expressed, that she had perhaps found someone who cared about her, who might even be reliable, *consistent.* Had Godot arrived?

The following session she arrived in a rage, throwing tissue boxes, knocking books to the floor. She exclaimed, 'I thought *wrongly* that you would understand and help with what was killing me ... but instead I have found my enemy. And if you think you'll get away with this you're *wrong,* you son of a bitch!'

My colleague stood there, silently stunned, the patient fuming.

Nothing to be done.

Or is there?

*****

To ameliorate the occasional slog, even the loneliness of the work, I often seek kinship with both analytic and literary works which salve the kind of fraught situatedness I am describing: an articulation of existential *angst*, lyrical consolation for unmet longing and daily struggle, in and out of the consulting room. Beckett's *oeuvre* provides a 'relational home' for me in this regard, especially when analysis comes to feel 'radically isolating' (Stolorow, 2011, p. 77).

In this chapter I discuss how Beckett's landmark play offers not only a potential way of seeing and even helping with the 'Godot' phenomenon in analysis, while pointing the way toward a kinship-in-finitude. Beckett's biography, too, adds to my intersubjective resonance (Stolorow & Atwood, 2016) with an author who describes life's existential plodding with reliably deep pathos and wit.

It is Beckett's illumination—poetic, empathic, humorous—of the darker corners of human relatedness and existence that inspires hope; his bleakly witty perspective becomes a tonic, for this analyst at least, especially when a dyadically foggy 'nothing' or 'nowhereness' settles in, and consolation is sorely needed.

***

Nothing is more real than nothing.

(Beckett, 1958a, p. 186)

For those who do not know or recall, the globally popular 'Godot' has a 'plot' which is simplicity itself: two forsaken tramps, Vladimir and Estragon (nicknamed Didi and Gogo, respectively)—physically ailing, in rags—linger beside a dusty road, under a spindly, leafless tree. They wait for Godot, apparently a respectable landowner, upon whom our tramps pin all hopes of redemption. While waiting (and waiting), they amuse and torment each other, with witty asides about their predicament, the impossibility of giving up—while driven mad by fruitless repetition.

They also, and this is a point sometimes missed by critics, each struggle with the frightful prospect of being left behind by the other, should that other leave or kill himself, as is sometimes considered. This theme of abandonment perseverates throughout Beckett's work, including in his other renowned play, *Endgame* (1958).

As Gogo remarks, 'Wouldn't it be better if we were to part?' Didi responds, 'You wouldn't go far' (p. 11).

They need each other, but resent each other for it, as 'neediness' is itself organized—as with many of our patients—as confirmation of their lowly status. I recall one patient, for instance, who remarked early in treatment, 'All my life I've been waiting for someone to tell me I'm okay.' Before I could respond to such poignancy, he collapsed into a pensive self-loathing which foreclosed further discussion.

Meanwhile our tramps teeter on the edge of despair or collapse, each of them occasionally threatening to exit. Such potential abandonment is actually more frightful than Godot's absence, leading me to wonder if the key function of waiting is that even the 'nothingness' of such circular activity *gives them something to do together:* a void-filling purpose.

Often, I find this to be the case with patients in apparently 'dead end' relationships; repetitively numbing or disappointing, yes, but at least *someone is there.* Sometimes in analyses as well, during difficult times when the patient is at least showing up—better than nothing, it would seem.

Death is also a common preoccupation in Beckett's work; here it is desired almost eagerly by the tramps (another dry irony), as a relief from tedium. Early in act one, the enlivening prospect of suicide—'Let's hang ourselves immediately!' exclaims Gogo—is dampened when they discover the skeletal tree can support only one noose, meaning one will be left behind, as the fortunate other enters eternal sleep. The idea is scotched, leaving a darkly comical resentment between them.

They continue to distract themselves, sustained engagement ever deflated by Godot's absence. 'I'd laugh if it weren't prohibited,' says Vladimir, his bladder aching. Estragon's feet are blistered; signs of a hobbled mobility. Another key theme emerges, related to traumatic aftermath: the 'fusion' of the developmental and the repetitive dimensions of self-experiencing (Stolorow & Atwood, 1992), where no sooner does hope appear—of Godot's possible appearance—than it is quashed immediately by disappointment, since Godot is (again) not coming.

Thus the play's circular, self-canceling movement, where waiting defines our tramps; it is, again, better than nothingness. (Probably.)

In the meantime they quibble like a long-married couple, over stinky boots, flatulence and garlicky breath, embodiments of a 'fallen' destiny. Such tumble from grace is also only inferred; remarks Vladimir, 'Hand in hand from the top of the Eiffel Tower.... We were respectable in those days. Now it's too late' (p. 7).

In each of the play's two acts, they are surprised by another wandering dyad, the blustering Pozzo and his man-servant, Lucky, the latter continually insulted, degraded and, in act one, about to be sold at market. (Beckett claimed he chose this name because 'he is Lucky to have no more expectations' (Bair, 1990, p. 384).) Yet to Pozzo's exasperation and Lucky's silent despair, they too cannot part: a more extreme version of the tramps' inter-dependence and mutual prickliness.

The tramps wait for an offstage Godot for rescue; Pozzo and Lucky rely concretely on each other, an accommodative relationship *in extremis*. Each seeks to fulfill an absurdly rigid self-ideal of control (Pozzo) and dependence (Lucky) in the hope of foreclosing risk of abandonment completely: each reifies the other as *absolutely* possessive (Pozzo) or 'owned' (Lucky), a riddance fantasy sprung to life. The impossibility of such fantasy's fulfillment leads to increasingly chaotic repetition, illustrated by Beckett's edgy slapstick. (In childhood Beckett loved the films of Chaplin, the Marx Brothers and so on. As did I.)

This second pair's frantic, even violent attempts to enact such a fantasy, result in abuse, both verbal and physical ('Pleasant evening we're having,' Vladimir quips, in the midst of all this), and eventually maim the participants; in the middle of act two they re-appear, now literally disabled in ways that manifest the unspoken psychological dilemma: Pozzo is blind, Lucky mute. Pozzo remarks wistfully, 'The blind have no notion of time.' A poetically deft touch on Beckett's part, as it not only points to the crippled reflectivity that comes with such rigidly repetitive circumvention of one's own vulnerability or trauma-pain, but also shows the cost of compulsive aversion to such affective exposure or 'weakness' while awaiting the other's *absolute* provision. In a way, such Brandchaftian repetition is already a kind of blindness, a loss of continuous self-experiencing via a disembodied, obsessive focus on a (concretely) redeeming other.

An air of sadness descends as the second pair staggers away, leaving our original twosome, who likely see a reflection of their own somewhat softer emotional aversions and relational entanglements in the broken-down pair now hobbling off. Still, they cannot help but await salvation.

Here they are again visited by a farmhand for Godot, the young brother of the boy who came earlier to deliver the same news: Godot is not coming, at least not today.

VLADIMIR: (to the boy): You don't know me? ... It wasn't you came yesterday?
(p. 33)

Godot's non-appearance again reflects their skeletal existence, a barely there-ness that, like Pozzo and Lucky (albeit not as extreme), obscures or collapses time—the stubborn return to a possibly pointless, unmet yearning. They fleetingly reconsider suicide, postponing again. Why not wait, since Godot may yet arrive ... tomorrow.

Estragon's ill-fitting trousers sag to his ankles while Vladimir struggles with his crumpled hat; destitute clowns in twilight.

VLADIMIR: Tomorrow, when I wake, what shall I say of today? That with Estragon ... until the fall of night, I waited for Godot? ... Probably. But in all that what truth will there be?
(p. 58)

One of the ways which 'Godot' parallels the clinical situation is its *befindlichkeit* (Heidegger, quoted in Gendlin, 1978–79)—or the encompassing mood of a given context—which, in this case, signifies the flattening aftermath of unnamed trauma.

The tramps accept the inflicting of such violence with equanimity. 'Did they beat you?' asks Vladimir early on. 'Of course they beat me!' Estragon exclaims. This is merely 'how things are.'

Meanwhile rescue or redemption remains in the wings: 'He'll save us,' remarks Vladimir, of the titular character, who will likely never appear (while just around the corner). A kind of dissociated uncanniness (Stolorow, 2015) prevails; they remain, like traumatized patients, 'outside' of life, looking in: a skeletal affectivity. I recall a patient who responded quite sincerely, when I asked her early in treatment how she found meeting in person versus speaking on the phone, 'Is there a difference?' An undoubtedly Beckettian response.

In uncanniness, time stands still; our tramps cannot agree on what day it is, how long they have waited. Similarly, my patient, like many others, often forgot how long she had been in analysis, or waiting for her boyfriend to leave his unhappy marriage. (There are also parallels in regard to social justice, with marginalized or aggressed communities fed up with waiting for some basic, humane recognition.)

Such frustratingly circular movement is still preferable with another; *someone,* at least, bears witness, even if that someone is equally woesome. Another can, after all, share a fantasy, lending it some semblance of validity. In analysis too, we may doubt or even frown upon a patient's fantasy of rescue, or riddance, while waiting for the right moment to address such notions; a 'collusion' of sorts, sometimes inevitable.

Thus, the developmental strives neck in neck with the repetitive. Beckett, for example, implies Godot may *not* be benign, a brute instead of savior, much as abusive caregivers—and later analysts—are experienced by patients as having two or more 'sides.'

In early drafts of the play, it was implied Pozzo *was* Godot (Bair, 1990), until Beckett decided that he wanted the play to be 'striving all the time to avoid definition' (Bair, 1990, p. 385), wary as he was of self-disclosure. Still, the tramps mistake Pozzo for Godot, and it is not clear they are mistaken. *Of course they beat me!*

Here change is hoped to be titrated, *known,* to some degree at least—while leaning too hard on certainty can lead to deflation, the collapse of hope. I see this when a patient's partner is addicted; the only thing more frightening than the partner never getting sober is … their getting sober, since patients intuit their own strivings will likely *remain unsatisfied,* until the partner seeks more fundamental change beyond either party's imaginings or experience. Thus, life with *and without* the partner is unimaginable. *Wouldn't it be better if we were to part?*

We analysts too, in such situations, face uncomfortable uncertainty, including whether or not our patients are willing to remain through inevitable disappointment, or relational turbulence. We do not always know whether or how analysis will work, what uncovered and possibly shameful trauma of our own will affect the dyad, what a patient's self-protections will look or feel like. We attempt to 'walk the tightrope' (Stolorow & Atwood, 2016) between knowing and not knowing, since we need a 'good enough' certainty in 'the process' while unavoidably uncertain about 'this' process.

Disillusionment, too, is often inevitable, since whatever 'Godot' a patient starts out desiring will likely never arrive; our version may not, either, at least in the way we imagine, or how or when; this may provoke some of our own prereflective, archaically unvalidated (Stolorow & Atwood, 1992) feelings of neglect or devaluation.

Yet it seems all-too-human, as Beckett illustrates, to desire or chase the impossible: our quixotic quest for all-encompassing outcomes, subtle or dramatic ... even as such pursuits or hopes cannot, in the end, evade finitude.

In this sense, then, both we and our patients *will always be waiting.*

> My resolutions were remarkable in this, that they were no sooner formed than something always happened to prevent their execution.
>
> (Beckett, 1955, p. 27)

We seek to help our patients survive existential crumbling, especially when it begins to sink in for them that any possible Godot will likely be symbolic rather than literal. Self-integration too, walks the tightrope, in being both liberating *and* painful. The latter, however, may seem impossible to patients enslaved to Brandchaftian relational ties.

In a sense, then, analysis—especially with patients who have relied on hope of a concretized Godot, ritualized self-protection, for years if not decades—*begins* at impasse. After all, subjective zones of self-experience, so historically terrifying to patients, *are precisely what we analysts value*, want to edge a patient towards and *through* rather than *around:* the 'mortar' of relational home-building—and, a patient often intuits, the most unbearable experience on the face of the earth.

For it is 'pain *that has to be experienced alone*' which becomes 'lastingly traumatic' (Stolorow, 2015, p. 125, italics mine)—and dangerous to revisit, compounded by compulsively repetitive numbing. But since trauma-affect 'that is held in a context of human understanding can gradually become more bearable' (p. 125), the uncovering of such affect is *our* Godot, and the anti-Godot for patients, who may feel the new context is potentially fatal (and can be, in part, in cases of addiction or suicidal depression). We too face risk, in attempting to guide a patient to safer ground, as we become invested, even as they oscillate towards and away from us.

ESTRAGON: I can't go on like this.
VLADIMIR: That's what *you* think.

(p. 60)

I cannot see how such struggle, foregrounded or otherwise, can fail to impact our vulnerabilities, and blind spots, meaning our own subjectivity remains 'by no means [a] settled issue' (Brandchaft, 2010, p. 198). Most of us are dedicated and passionate about the work. Yet it can be a grueling process that requires us, too, to stretch and evolve, changing within the process and with the patient. No two relationships are alike, implying the brushing up against the unknown, the edgily prereflective, in unforeseen ways, repeatedly.

Consider, as one example, the discomfort felt when we sense having to 'step outside' our chosen theory, potentially disappointing peers, mentors or supervisors 'watching from the wings'; their approval may be one of *our* Godots, their disapproval the frightful opposite. How to differentiate from such transferential figures is but one way an analyst 'likely *also* [has] to undergo a painful process of realignment … in the focus of his interpretive activity' (Brandchaft, 1994, p. 60).

In some difficult instances, I find a patient's defensive process manifesting as a riddance fantasy, or 'affective purification' (Stolorow, 2015, p. 125), reflecting an archaically-derived contempt or devaluation of emotionality itself, which is after all the investigative center of my chosen theory! This, together with the asymmetry of analysis, parallels my earlier 'gifted child' situation, possibly provoking a killer-organizing centered around my historic fear of inadequacy. *Pig!*

Such fear creates a heightened apprehension when the patient 'exits,' literally if not affectively: the result of my shameful limitations. A mutually pervasive 'shameworld' may take hold (Orange, 2008, p. 97). A patient's urgent need for certainty and 'direction,' from 'the professional,' becomes a dark attractor state (Thelen & Smith, 1994) pulling me into a kind of fraught non-relational home disconcertingly familiar.

Such 'entrapment' often feels like a Pozzo/Lucky dynamic with no alternatives—as in feeling forced to accommodate *a patient's* demanding, Pozzo-like other, who requires proof of 'progress,' non-delivery of which is potentially fatal to the patient, who remains convinced he needs the other's approval to survive. Such a fraught belief may be, again, intellectually 'untrue,' while *felt* to be authentic, when the patient has no real memory of surviving archaic abandonments or annihilating attacks (Winnicott, 1974).

POZZO: (to tramps): You seem human, more or less.

(p. 15)

It is sometimes a lonely business. Another reason I find inspiration in both Beckett's work and his biography, as from the ashes of his own traumatic history he created a witty, lasting art, testament to the power of creativity itself—as we ourselves aspire to co-create a new relatedness from the ashes of both participants' trauma, and from the 'rubble' of enactments, impasses or other dyadic implosions.

It is hard for me to not see Beckett as heroic for the mere fact of his resistance activity during the Nazi occupation of Paris, however humble he was about it later (if he mentioned it at all). His modesty was overstated; his secret translations and ferrying documents were enough to draw the suspicion of the Gestapo, forcing him to flee to the countryside. He returned after the war to a ghost-city purged of its best and brightest. (The enactment of one of history's most notorious riddance fantasies.) He missed his friends terribly—some of whom were in hiding, while others had perished in the camps.

At the same time, this period marks the beginning of his arguably best writing, including 'Godot.' His creativity, in fact, kept him from falling apart; while on the run Beckett, along with his long-time companion Suzanne, remained in hiding in the countryside, where he forced himself to uphold a writing schedule to stay sane (Bair, 1990). The result was *Watt,* one of his more accessible novels.

During this period, he and his fellow 'tramp' lacked basic provisions, often hungry or cold for days, until such basics arrived. It was, psychologically at least, a situation for which his upbringing had prepared him.

'Godot' brought Beckett fame and fortune, freeing him to write full-time. Yet this long-awaited fame was also disappointing, as the 'Godot' he *actually* craved was not the one that arrived; he felt his fiction and later play, *Endgame,* were superior, and became dismissive of admiration of 'Godot,' even calling it 'a bad play' (Bair, 1990, p. 388). The recognition he awaited proved elusive, something those of us with authorial aspirations of our own may understand. Even winning the Nobel Prize led him to feel yet more, per the title of Knowlson's (1996) biography, 'damned to fame.' True to character, he gave away his prize money to struggling friends, especially artists and writers.

***

It all started, as always, at home. Beckett survived a tumultuous childhood in Foxrock, near Dublin, which he was all too happy to flee after college.[1] His mother May was what we might today call 'bi-polar,' as strict and managerial as Beckett's father was benignly anarchic. May's moods swung unpredictably; Beckett and his older brother Frank used to hide from her beneath the dining room table, waiting for father Bill's arrival. Once home, May berated him for any number of reasons; one imagines quite a few Pozzo-like tirades. Bair (1990) remarks that May's temper caused young Beckett nightmares and fear of the dark; much of his fiction attempts to illuminate such fraught and fearful darkness.

His father remained earthy and celebratory of 'swearing, farting and belching' (Bair, 1990, p. 23–24), before mother once again intruded. Is this childhood cycle of joy and terror the inspiration for the 'infinitizing of finitude, the circular ordering of chaos' (Stolorow, 2011, p. 58) we encounter in Beckett's writings? *Wouldn't it be better if we were to part?* One of Beckett's later novels, *The Unnamable* (1958b), features a narrator trapped in a jar, the fractured musings of a vague 'someone' who is not sure how to narrate his life story, if anyone including the narrator would even find it interesting. (Unlikely.) Beckett's writing often carries the pensive air of a person staving off dread or despair, offering anecdotes and quips before gloom again sets in.

Like many of our patients, Beckett felt agonizingly torn between his parents:

> There was guilt for loving their father so much when their mother told them repeatedly how disgraceful was his behavior; there was shame that they loved him who was so bad and hated her who was so good.... These emotions ... became the source of severe mental anguish ... and found their way repeatedly into his writings.
>
> (Bair, 1990, p. 24)

Thus the forging of an impossibly paradoxical tornness; even after fleeing to Paris, largely to escape his mother and find an expansive new life, he remained nagged by guilt about leaving his family behind.

In 1934, Beckett sought analysis with a young Wilfred Bion at the Tavistock Clinic (Knowlson, 1996). He claimed Bion's most helpful intervention was an invitation to hear a talk by C.G. Jung; in this talk Jung mentioned a patient whose dreams revealed that 'she was never born entirely' (Bair, 1990, p. 209).

Beckett seized on the remark as 'the keystone to his entire analysis,' serving as explanation of his 'womb fixation' and 'all of his behavior,' including the bed-ridden depressions that followed 'frequent visits to his mother' (all quotes, p. 209).

The metaphor resonates for our purposes as well. Our tramps—like many of our patients, even ourselves—often appear 'half-born,' or half-*there,* oscillating between hope and disappointment in equal measure. An addiction becomes but one compelling way of numbing such insidious subjective tornness (Atwood, 2012), a companion that makes waiting for redemption palatable, even as it postpones any *actual,* authentic growth.

An analyst's 'Godot,' in this context, becomes an empathic midwife of sorts, 'delivering' a patient's selfhood half-stuck in the womb. Anxiety results when inevitable 'labor pains' such as enactments or impasses become repetitively protracted for uncertain reasons or duration—resulting in a terror of botching the job, leaving a patient's hopes stillborn yet again. *Let's hang ourselves immediately!*

I have had to ask myself what of my own subjectivity leads to these types of fears, or grip of a patient's requirement to remain omni-attuned to, not only the patient, but the significant others in the patient's relational system—where love is synonymous with accommodation, twinship ever nullified in favor of one's being Lucky *or* Pozzo. What of my *own* prereflective anxiety co-creates such concretized or antidotal pressure?

Here Beckett's biography is again instructive. For he never quite forgave himself for abandoning his family, especially brother Frank, who he used to protect from his mother's blows. Shortly after 'Godot' brought Beckett the freedom to write full-time, he lost his brother to a fast-metastasizing cancer.

(His mother had died shortly before, his father before that.) The last of his immediate family was suddenly, traumatically *gone*, sending Beckett into one of his worst depressions; here he 'railed at the unfairness of it all, and berated himself ... as being somehow responsible' (Bair, 1990, p. 445).

Like Beckett, I too had a younger sibling with whom I hid and played with, amidst perpetual emotional storms. My sister Andrea, two years my junior, was my original Estragon. Having her for twinship made childhood far more palatable. Even into adulthood we held onto our inside jokes and stories.

Except that she died from her escalating addiction several years ago (this is hard to write)—a loss I continue to mourn. Her own relentless addiction was a 'Pozzo' long feared and loathed, and fully removed from my influential reach.

Such loss came, along with losing my father two years previously, after the arrival of long-awaited success, in starting my own practice. I occasionally wonder if I did enough to help her, considering my vocation—a complex grieving process ever unfolding, which I plan to explore further in subsequent writings. Suffice it to say for now that repetitive gloom once again closely shadowed forward movement, familiar yet newly, unspeakably tragic.

POZZO: They give birth astride a grave, the light gleams an instant, then it's night once more.

(p. 57)

I can't go on, I'll go on.

(Beckett, 1958b, p. 407)

This is why I find it crucial to remain a patient as well as an analyst, as it is often the very things I dread—enactments or other painful repetitions—that show me precisely where I need to 'stretch.' I am, after all, asking precisely this from my patients.

Earlier in my career, I imagined it necessary to keep the affective aftermath of my own historic trauma 'out of the process,' lest I project upon the patient, as if I could somehow erase *aspects of my own subjectivity*: an absurd impossibility, no matter how vigilant I remained. Such self-imposed erasure reflects some of my own subjective demands to accommodate archaic Pozzos: it is the residue of *their* influence, in fact, that needs curbing! Understanding the persistence of such subjective influence cultivates compassion for patients' Brandchaftian ties to archaic Pozzos of their own.

It is only human, furthermore, to find appealing those twinships with patients that come with a playfulness and humor akin to what I enjoyed with Andrea; finitude, it would seem, includes the acceptance of affective vulnerability, rather than viewing it as a contaminant within the dyadic. Analytic alliances may or may not survive, though the yearning cannot and probably *should* not be eliminated; humility need not be humiliation, in regard to self-awareness. Humor and playfulness can be healing, even expansive, for patients who too had to grow up fast, prematurely foreclosing transitional space (Winnicott, 1965).

In short, there is no escaping the distinctly existential vulnerabilities within our situatedness, the 'own-ness' of our own traumatic history (Stolorow, 2007). The deeper and more empathically we understand such influence, in accepting our own finitude, the more fully we allow ourselves to be present with others, in our hope of helping them become more fully born. This, from where I stand now, is as close as I can come to defining but one type of dyadically discovered Godot.

In fact it is the acceptance of my own vulnerability to loss, and *anxious anticipation of possible loss,* that cultivates a kinship-in-mourning with patients who have lost irreplaceable others, along with aspects of their own child-selves, forever unrecoverable; we analysts, good as we may be, cannot reverse time. However, acknowledging to patients the impact of my mistakes and ways in which I may have disappointed them, difficult as this can be, fosters analytic expansiveness, disconfirming the expectation that a patient's self-experiencing will once again be invalidated (Stolorow & Atwood, 1992).

Important, too, that I continue to recognize the potential threat of the new alliance, where patients may sense (often shamefully) that in differentiating, they are abandoning those they were or are responsible for protecting, namely Pozzo-like caregivers—past or transferential—that I might perceive as abusive; such figures remain part of the tender own-ness of patients' own histories, with the shame of loving those that others in their life frown upon.

POZZO: I woke up one fine day as blind as Fortune. (pause) I sometimes wonder if I'm not still asleep.

(p. 57)

There is another way in which reflecting both on my sister's death, and Beckett's thematic explorations of death, has illuminated my own anxiety over the possible 'death' of an analysis, when a patient affectively withdraws, temporarily or permanently, as one of my first analytic patients did not long ago, via the most cursory of texts.

The Atwoodian (2015) scenario of being prematurely responsible to care for our own caregivers, may have left *us* in a half-born state, always awaiting psychic completion, in any and all types of relatedness, analytic or otherwise.

To lose, in other words, a chance for our *own* expansiveness, in and out of our role as analyst, is a loss that can echo other losses: a kind of domino effect than can become overwhelming. Losing my sister, for instance, threw trauma from my childhood into starker relief, since it was my kinship with her that ameliorated unspeakable pain and isolation.

Some of us 'little psychotherapists' have, like our patients, learned to do a lot with very little. I recall how, at the age of seven, after losing my grandfather, troubled by the violence I was exposed to in movies and television, I experienced a panicky terror of death, which I envisioned one awful night as a permanent, unalterable and *fully conscious* isolation.

I could not discuss such terrors with my parents, for fear of being mocked or minimized: a bone-gripping terror of a *symbolically* unacknowledged death already occurring in the milieu; my nightmarish image of a disembodied consciousness was a concretization of the unbearable isolation ever present—an unacknowledged thirst for intersubjectively-thwarted understanding.

I am reminded of Kohut's (1982) touching description of death as 'the loss of an empathic milieu' (p. 397); in some parentified child scenarios, for patients and analysts alike, it may be more accurate to say 'the loss of a *potentially attuned or empathic milieu*,' since 'the child's own development ... has been interrupted and frozen' (Atwood, 2015, p. 151).

In other words, losing the other comes to signify a loss of selfhood, or *potential* for expansion, and ongoing non-recognition of developmental desire, repetitively foreclosed integration. We come to embody such an opportunity for patients, a restoratively expansive way of Being-with, when we pursue such healing relatedness *ourselves*, passing it on as it were—another possible dyadic 'Godot.'

In the case of my colleague and his angry client ('you son of a bitch!') it was a matter of understanding how closely her yearning and trauma-pain were intertwined. As the patient's trust of the analyst grew, so did her mistrust and the emergence of long-sequestered pain. (With the developmental comes the repetitive; whatever is expansive grows a shadow.) Eventually such pain, a long-averted psychic wound, exploded into expression.

What provoked this detonation was a change of footwear; my colleague had, prior to her outburst, worn sandals, a kind of savior or Christ-like allusion. His switch to loafers triggered rage in a patient whose emotional reservoir was already close to bursting; it signaled he would *not* be her savior, her tantalizing glimpse of Godot again foreclosed.

My colleague, too, suffered a lost childhood (Atwood, 2015); this type involves the sudden loss of a caregiver, which the 'little psychotherapist' then replaces. In this case the analyst's Godot was a rescue-fantasy based on his *becoming* and thus replacing the lost parent for his patient's abandoned child-self. This analyst generally leaned more toward developmental, forward edge (Tolpin, 2002) interventions, in hope of facilitating a patient's self-expansion. It was her nerve-rattling explosions that dramatically showed him a more affectively inclusive Godot was needed, requiring his accepting *all* of her, the sweet and the sour, as such primal self-experiencing had been long forbidden.

She needed him to witness, in other words, her existential howl of protest—provoked initially by a minor change in his appearance, a symbolic abandonment by the (symbolically) loving father—in order to know that he would indeed be able to facilitate a healing, for a selfhood gripped by demands for accommodation, the sequestering of existence-pain. In doing so he struggled, with the help of peer consultation and a few stiff drinks, to tolerate the fear of being an 'anti-Godot,' as roughly twenty more explosions followed, over ten years of treatment. Since then there has been a decade of self-consolidation, both of them settling in to a shared *there*-ness.

Who am I to tell my private nightmares to if I can't tell them to you?

Not only does this story illuminate my colleague's patience and commitment to understanding a patient's subjectivity, it also reassures me that we never 'graduate,' that we all need support from time to time, whether it be peers, analysts, martinis, or a dose of Beckettian vaudeville.

The great adventure of analysis, then, consists of the transformation and maintenance—for *both* participants, in ways overt and subtle—from Godot into 'Godot,' from the literal to the symbolic/affective. Such clarity sometimes emerges only after participants survive a co-occurring enactment or impasse, overcast giving way to broadened clarity. It is as if patients need to know the relationship can survive an attack of intertwined killer organizing, in order to safely proceed.

It is also the case, for better and worse, that some patients need to leave treatment—more than once, even—before they can truly begin. This is especially true for those coerced into analysis or therapy by an impatient other, where the desired change is mechanical or behavioral, rather than the genuine loosening of antidotal or ritualized numbing of painful affect, of Brand-chaftean accommodation. Such patients are so accustomed to being Lucky that, in order to feel whole, a decision can only be theirs if they either 'rebel' by fleeing, or treating others—often unwittingly—with Pozzo-like imperiousness, to (concretely) rebalance the psychological scales. Then they may return, a decision that is *theirs*. When or if they will do so remains, of course, an open question.

In the meantime, we wait.

VLADIMIR: Well, shall we go?
ESTRAGON: Yes, let's go.

They do not move.
CURTAIN

(p. 60)

Note

1 He once remarked that he preferred wartime France to peace-time Ireland (Kenner, 1968).

References

Atwood, G.E. (2012). *The abyss of madness*. New York: Routledge.

Atwood, G.E. (2015). Credo and reflections. *Psychoanalytic Dialogues*, 25: 137–152.

Bair, D. (1990). *Beckett: a biography*. New York: Summit Books.

Beckett, S. (1954). *Waiting for Godot*. New York: Grove Press.

Beckett, S. (1955). *Molloy*. New York: Grove Press.

Beckett, S. (1958). *Endgame*. New York: Grove Press.

Beckett, S. (1958a). *Malone Dies*. New York: Grove Press.

Beckett, S. (1958b). *The Unnamable*. New York: Grove Press.

Brandchaft, B. (2010). Systems of pathological accommodation in psychoanalysis. In B. Brandchaft, S. Doctors, & D. Sorter, *Toward an emancipatory psychoanalysis: Brandchaft's intersubjective vision* (pp. 193–220). New York: Routledge.

Brandchaft, B. (1994). To free the spirit from its cell. In R.D. Stolorow, G.E. Atwood, & B. Brandchaft (Eds.), *The intersubjective perspective* (pp. 57–74). Northvale, NJ: Jason Aronson Inc.

Brothers, D. (2008). *The trauma of uncertainty: Trauma-centered psychoanalysis*. New York: Analytic Press.

Coburn, W.J. (2002). A world of systems: The role of systemic patterns of experience in the therapeutic process. *Psychoanalytic Inquiry*, 22: 655–677.

Ferenczi, S. (1932/1988). *The clinical diary of Sandor Ferenczi*, J. Dupont (Ed.). Cambridge: Harvard University Press.

Gendlin, E. (1978–79). Befindlichkeit: Heidegger and the philosophy of psychology. *Review of Existential Psychology & Psychiatry: Heidegger and Psychology*, 16(1–3): 43–71.

Kenner, H. (1968). *Samuel Beckett: A critical study*. Berkeley, CA: University of California Press.

Knowlson, J. (1996). *Damned to fame: The life of Samuel Beckett*. New York: Simon & Schuster.

Kohut, H. (1982). Introspection, empathy, and the semi-circle of mental health. *International Journal of Psycho-Analysis*, 63: 395–407.

Lichtenberg, J.D. (1999). Listening, understanding and interpreting: Reflections on complexity. *International Journal of Psycho-Analysis*, 80: 719–737.

Miller, A. (1997). *The drama of the gifted child*. New York: Basic Books.

Orange, D.M. (2006). For whom the bell tolls: Context, complexity, and compassion in psychoanalysis. *International Journal of Psychoanalytic Self Psychology*, 1: 5–21.

Orange, D.M. (2008). Whose shame is it anyway?: Lifeworlds of humiliation and systems of restoration (Or, 'The Analyst's Shame'). *Contemporary Psychoanalysis*, 44: 83–100.

Orenstein, A. (1995). The fate of the curative fantasy in the psychoanalytic treatment process. *Contemporary Psychoanalysis*, 31: 113.

Stolorow, D.S. & Stolorow, R.D. (1987) Affects and selfobjects. In *Psychoanalytic treatment: An intersubjective approach* (pp. 66–87). Hillsdale, NJ: The Analytic Press.

Stolorow, R.D. (1993). Thoughts on the nature and therapeutic action of psychoanalytic interpretation. *Progress in Self Psychology*, 9: 31–43.

Stolorow, R.D. (1999). Antidotes, enactments, rituals, and the dance of reassurance: Comments on the case of Joanna Churchill & Alan Kindler. *Progress in Self-Psychology*, 15: 229–232.

Stolorow, R.D. (2007). *Trauma and human existence*. New York: The Analytic Press.

Stolorow, R.D. (2011). *World, affectivity, trauma: Heidegger and post-Cartesian psychoanalysis*. New York: Routledge.

Stolorow, R.D. (2015). A phenomenological-contextual, existential, and ethical perspective on emotional trauma. *Psychoanalytic Review*, 102: 123–138.

Stolorow, R.D. & Atwood, G.E. (1992). *Contexts of being: The intersubjective foundations of psychological life*. Hillsdale, NJ: The Analytic Press.

Stolorow, R.D. & Atwood, G.E. (2016). Walking the tightrope of emotional dwelling. *Psychoanalytic Dialogues*, 26: 103–108.

Stolorow, R.D., Atwood, G.E., & Orange, D.M. (1997). *Working intersubjectively: Contextualism in psychoanalytic practice*. Hillsdale, NJ: The Analytic Press.

Thelen, E. & Smith, L. (1994). *A dynamic systems approach to the development of cognition and action*. Cambridge, MA: MIT Press.

Tolpin, M. (2002). Doing psychoanalysis of normal development: Forward edge transferences. *Progress in Self Psychology*, 18: 167–190.

Winnicott, D.W. (1965). *The maturational processes and the facilitating environment: Studies in the theory of emotional development*. London: The Hogarth Press.

Winnicott, D.W. (1974). Fear of breakdown. *International Review of Psycho-Analysis*, 1: 103–107.

Chapter 2

The Doorknob Dilemma

Introduction

The question grabbed me and did not let go. Even after she left, it lingered.

'Is she gonna be ok, Darren?'

I asked myself the same question. Yes or no? *Which is it, Doc?*

If nature abhors a vacuum, analysis abhors a binary. Yet my patient, Linda, seemed to need a 'fix,' or antidote, like everyone in her family. I understood Linda's terror even as her question itself reflected the problem, stoking the binary that led to the question that led to the binary ...

It was early going for us. Still.... *Yes or no, Mr. Fancy Degree?*

A sense of dread settled in, as I could either a) answer or b) disappoint her. She wanted that opiate of a response so she could relax and return to serving her husband, her daughter, even the dog, who got his walk or treat the moment he barked.

C'mon Doc, she's waitin'!

On the other hand, I sensed (like an angel on the other shoulder) the 'analytic police' counseling me to explore, illuminate, empathize.

Sounds good on paper, Doc, but this here's the real world! Why not just give her the fix. Think your colleagues would do any different?

Would they?

At any rate it was up to me to steer the ship, in what was surely a long-term process. *Maybe a century, pardner.*

Linda seemed strictly uninterested in her own feelings, obsessing instead about the minutiae of her daughter's addiction (which she deeply feared her daughter might not survive). Linda would stand and pause, hand on the doorknob, pressing me for a last-minute response—as if I held a magic 8-ball: 'Will she make it?'

The answers of course lie beyond the binary, in some speechless realm: words found in the writing of this essay. By reflecting on our interactions and what might be happening, including my own pensive pessimism, I found it was

DOI: 10.4324/9781003266358-3

precisely this divisive experiencing that described the patient's world—and my own, in ways initially elusive.

Linda's question about her daughter, her only child, put to me with under a minute left in the game—together with her own unresolved, conflicted feeling-states—provoked my anxiety, eerily familiar.

My early world too was marked by emotional violence, as well as humor and playfulness followed again by volatile eruption—all underscored by demands to accommodate caregivers, so that such eruptions were 'airbrushed' out of history.

Sometimes we need to find ways to self-integrate, bring ourselves back together, in the midst of difficult treatments—recenter, via our own analysis or supervision or a creative process. This essay represents such an attempt, an explored synthesis of light and dark—transcending the tyranny of the either/or.

This Gun for Hire

> She was a quiet sorta dame, real mom next door type. Kept to herself, like she'd make herself invisible if she could. Her husband, real brute. Never met a cocktail he didn't like, and boy was he pushy. Loud and bullish, his way or the highway, you know the type. Why she didn't clock him is anyone's guess. It were me, I might've given him a nudge from behind, at the top of the stairs like, and oh lookie an accident! But not her. Hadda play it nice, good little girl in Sunday church, just like daddy wanted. Almost fell outta my chair when she asked why was she so blue. I'd be earnin' my lettuce on this one, every damn nickel.

This monologue, echoing the 'inner Bogie' above, is how I might begin the story of my treatment of Linda were I to adopt the Sam Spade/Philip Marlowe cool-as-marble persona I so enjoy in countless, hard-boiled noir movies and books. The movies I watched with my father; we loved the quips between Bogart and Bacall, the feisty stoicism of Cagney and Edgar G. Robinson, the throwaway lines before somebody got iced. A little later I discovered the books that kicked the whole thing off, Hammett, Chandler, Chester Himes (underrated), and others.

The cultural influence of noir is impossible to miss. How this well-established, influential genre might mesh with analytic theories I employ, especially Kohut and intersubjective-systems, is in part what inspired this essay.

It is the tough-guy, Bogart-like cynicism that attracts me, cigarette perched on the lips. The originators of noir had great impact on some of my existential heroes, including Camus and Sartre, as well as the films of Hitchcock, Godard, and Martin Scorsese. Even the likes of Beckett and Wittgenstein could not resist hard-boiled detectives. To quote Bogart is to reinvoke a world of nostalgia; my first and only (unpublished) novel featured an alcoholic psychoanalyst who seduces the girlfriend of a volatile patient. The plotline was Freud by way of Marlowe. *Here's looking at you, Id.*

This attraction to rain-slicked toughness stems both from my clinical work and personal experience with addiction: a mindset often characterized by a hard-edged, bottom-line attitude, even in recovery. The folk wisdom of Alcoholics Anonymous can be world weary, raw: 'fuck your feelings, just don't drink. Your ego ain't your amigo' and so on. As my 'inner Bogie' might say: 'Addiction'll snuff ya like a match in a hurricane.'

I cannot help but think at certain moments of psychoanalysis as existentially empathic detective work, exploring the 'clues' of a patient's affectivity, tracing the origins of such tumult and distress to the archaic crime scene. Which will have the upper hand in treating addiction: compulsive denial, self-destruction, or vulnerability? Some patients after all, daunted by the sometimes-grueling process of change, decide analysis is a waste or takes too long; perhaps EMDR is the surer bet. Some exit analysis abruptly, then later overdose or even kill themselves. This has happened with a few patients, after they faded away or bolted.

The crime scene is often an archaic 'murder,' the patient's innocence or authenticity 'rubbed out' by the (sometime violent) indifference of mis-attunement and caregivers' rigid self-interests, akin to that of a crime boss. A coverup then ensues to protect the powerful. The crime at the heart of many noirs, including Roman Polanski's film, *Chinatown*, is an incestuous transgression, as in this 1974 classic, where a tycoon, vividly portrayed by John Huston, impregnates his own daughter (played by Faye Dunaway), shocking an iconically cool detective played by Jack Nicholson, who has fallen for his doomed paramour.

I am often disturbed by what I hear in the consulting room. What frequently shocks is not just details of abusive intrusion or neglect, but the denial that follows, a numbing normalization—as in, 'there's no use dwelling in the past' or caregivers 'did the best they could.' *Gee, I'd hate to see their worst!*

We may wonder who or what is 'murdered' in an analytic case involving addiction and its shadowy twin, pathological accommodation (Brandchaft, 2010). I think we can take the cue from Shengold's (1989) *Soul Murder*, where it is the vital spontaneity and creativity of the child that is 'bumped off' day after normalized day. Usually there is no single incident, but rather a cruel ritualization of malattunement in serving the powers that be for an overburdened, parentified or gifted child (Miller, 1981). A most terrible dilemma is thus foisted upon the young one, a traumatic torn-ness (Atwood, 2011), as proved to be the case with Linda, past and present—no cakewalk, this case.

But wise guy comments do not a treatment make. In fact, they have tended to confuse me, even gumming up the works. It took the writing of this very chapter to figure out how the world-weary, Bogie'ish voice might get along with the more hopeful voices of self-psychology and intersubjective-systems theory. My mentors are often fond of saying, 'Analysis is a long road, years if not decades. Explore, illuminate, empathize.'

Blah blah blah. Most folks ain't got that kinda patience, or dough!

There is truth here to both, resulting in a subjective torn-ness of my own.

Many patients who struggle with addiction, or with an addicted loved one, are often (initially) resistant or unfamiliar with reflective processes. They remain aversive or numbed to their own emotionality, struggling to identify what 'feelings' are or how to name them, even as ruminative conceptualization remains very much alive, albeit isolating. Relationality here is seen as a Rubik's cube to 'figure out' how to navigate relatedness, a frustrating endeavor after being born and bred in a highly concretized world. In such scenarios emotionality is dangerous, as the vulnerability of the child is villainized, repeatedly under the bus. Analysis becomes a long-term CPR for patients who begin by praying that their inner kid simply plays dead, in the service of cognitive empowerment and in line with archaic ideals of self-sufficiency.

But the actual villain, most often a coverup of caregiver abuse or other relational crimes, remains stubbornly protected.

> *Yes, which is why all this fancy theory don't cut it. Folks wanna stay numb. Waking up to the hell of your life, a nightmare you can't escape … forget it! Better to stay zonked. Beats pullin' your hair out, on account of someone doesn't want the help. Too cynical, you say? Go on then, prove me wrong. I'm waitin' …*

The Jeopardy Theme

Linda arrives, a few minutes late, amiable and slightly tousled, in a sweatshirt and jeans, as if she's just rushed in from somewhere. She sits with the usual shy pensiveness, exchanges pleasantries with me, amiably chatting about some celebrity gossip viewed on television or on the pages of People. She enjoys it, as do I … for a few minutes, before the familiar uneasiness falls like a shadow. Trying to 'go deeper' goes nowhere.

The sun is peeping through the venetian blinds, casting striped shade on the wall, like a scene from a forties flick. This is the same sun Chandler observed in his memorable descriptions of Los Angeles, which he described as 'a city with the personality of a paper cup' (www.libquotes.com, n.d.). Sometimes the treatment with Linda feels the same. *And whose fault is that, Doctor?*

When Linda first arrived a few short months ago, she was both borderline suicidal and jumpier than oil on a hot skittle. She was eager for me to 'fix' her depression so she could get back to her housekeeping duties, rather than lie listlessly in bed, earning the hellish wrath of her husband, Alan. Alan is a borderline alcoholic, financially successful but agitated and demanding (as Linda's mother was and is), blaming his wife for his misery. Linda feels she has to simply 'take it' or maybe deserves it, her self-esteem in the gutter.

What stymies me among other things is her insistence that she is worthless and that she must serve her husband, Tom, who earns all the bread and therefore gets to inarguably 'call the shots.' This gnaws at me like a mouse on cheddar.

I fretted over her (my inner Jewish mother) in the early days as she repeatedly intoned, 'I just want out of all this.' Out, it sounded to me, of her own subjectivity! Full of self-hatred she was, convinced her husband and daughter were right and that her not 'snapping out of it' was sheer laziness, again inarguably.

Her daughter, Tammy, has been using opiates again, having taken a sabbatical (again) from college. Tammy is 25 and has yet to complete her undergraduate degree. Linda worries this is due to her depression, which Tammy seizes upon to defend her sleeping until evening, when again it's party time with friends: a result of Linda's 'garbage' mothering, a notion reinforced by Alan.

Over our first few anguished weeks, her depression lifted like June gloom. She had found, with her 'miracle-worker shrink,' a medication 'cocktail' that did wonders. She was sleeping better, a dreamless slumber that had eluded her. She said not word one to me about the alleviations of analysis, leading me to wonder if I was indeed chopped liver. But it was early yet, as I had been reminded so often during my candidacy. The road of analysis is long, full of dips and hills, best not to call attention to oneself like her self-centered, jerky husband and parents, etc., etc.

Her shambolic father was an alcoholic, demanding she stifle any criticism of him lest he explode. Now she describes a game they played, where she would mix and bring him martinis, sit on his lap and tell him about her day. Something about this gives me the willies, this 'game' stretching into her teen years. Maybe it's the way she dismisses it with a laugh, flinching mildly when relating her father's cracks about her weight (hurtful, to my ears) that she also laughs off. (In a Hitchcock film, such airiness would precede a manic breakdown.)

I say 'ouch' in regard to the wisecracks; she responds, 'he was just cranky' or 'that's just the booze talkin.' *Uh-huh ... and I got a bridge to sell ya.*

Now, the worst of her depression having lifted, she wants only to talk about ... nothing, really. Pleasantries, celebrity gossip, enjoyable nonsense. It is as if the pale-faced, anguished woman who first graced my doorway no longer exists, that plaintive concern, despair, and terror all erased in the most unsettling way. Here again I am torn. I almost miss that iteration of Linda; there was something so raw and authentic about it. Yet I'm relieved she feels better, and if she has no interest in her own ravaged psyche, what can I do? *As I said, Herr Doktor ...*

But it's too soon to give up, so today I ask again, with gentle indirectness, what happened to all that terror and pain. 'All gone,' she says, smiling like a little girl. Then the amiable chatter about the Kardashians: 'Can you believe she said that? Why are those two married?' (A question I sometimes ponder about her and her husband.)

She is witty and charming, I enjoy her poking fun at pompous politicians or celebrities, and it is all pleasant, like eating popcorn ... though popcorn come to think of it gives me nausea, a queasy feeling in the room now, the black and white shadow-rows of the blinds sinking with the sun, the earth rotating, life proceeding while we both prattle amiably as if we are at a murder scene, ignoring the chalked outline of a corpse. I get that 'don't-speak-of-the elephant-in-the-corner' feeling often found with patients in the grip of addictive chaos, a faint déjà vu I ought to pay closer attention to, flitting in and out of awareness like a mosquito. Bzzzz she goes, on and on, until I ask her like a dentist with his drill, hovering close to the cavity, how her daughter is doing.

She winces. A pained look. I hate doing this, but someone has to. She loves that anesthesia. I am tempted to say she is 'avoidant,' but maybe that's too pathologizing, more a reflection of *my* frustration. *But if the shoe fits, Doc ...* 'I need to get rid of this depression!' she has said repeatedly, a tortured mantra. Has she? Or has it been masked over, a cheap bandaid? I sense that my wanting to look at it is, for her, picking at the scab.

Just hang in there, another twenty years oughtta do it, heh heh ...

Linda slides away from the question, back to her daughter, who is claiming she goes to her 12-step meetings, therapy appointments, job interviews, who says she is sober ... even as she sleeps until late afternoon, leaving the kitchen a holy wreck after making herself a fashionably late dinner at three in the morning. She sometimes posts the wreckage on Instagram, captioned 'Late night mac and cheese LOL!'

Linda and Tammy do the dance of rage, guilt, repair. But it feels hollow to me; we've seen this movie a lot. Linda says she took the bait last night and asked Tammy for an update on her job search and recovery, her daughter exploding: 'Butt out! I'm an adult!' Linda responded, 'Start acting like one!' This was followed by her, Linda's, guilty collapse, an extra 'Xanny' for sleep. Linda now chastises herself, in the late afternoon shadows, about her own 'cruelty' to Tammy, her indifference to her husband, who complains about not having sex in months—as if he's asking her to do the dishes. *Hey lady, how can you want to boff a guy who treats you like a dog?* As is so typical of a former gifted child, her 'failings' preoccupy her. She fears acting like her mother, who nitpicked her to death as a child. Linda resented it and couldn't wait to leave for college. Is she doing the same to Tammy? Sometimes I say, 'I doubt it.' Nothing gets through.

What bugs me is that what I think doesn't seem to matter or have impact. She may take in a little of it, but all of it seems forgotten by next session.

We often get stuck in the minutiae of her daughter's appointments and progress and drug use ... next to nothing about Linda herself, as if dwelling there even momentarily is sinful. She cannot stay with a feeling to save her life (and maybe she had to do this in childhood, to save her life). Here is the elephant again, but we cannot talk about it, no matter my efforts. *Twenty years, eh Doc?*

Then, as Linda heads for the door, she pauses with her hand on the doorknob and says, 'Tell me she's gonna be okay.'

I am surprised, though she has after all asked this a few times. Still I'm on the spot again, a pop quiz. Yes or no? A push-pull, tick tock ...

Answering feels like giving in, while silence leaves her stranded, both of us now riven in place, a gnawing sense of inadequacy and irritation like the proverbial frog in the simmering pot, a moment where to say goodbye was to really feel the heat.

The Big Somewhere

We process it. Explore and examine it from all angles, me with questions such as, 'What makes you ask? What's it like when I answer or don't? What's the price of tea in China?'

Nothing helps, no matter how often we go over it (and minimally even then). She still presses me with the question, the pop quiz, every third or fourth session. Often, I am hesitant to bring it up the following day.

Perhaps it is because I have no answer but 'ought to.' I also resent this while reminding myself that I am the one with the degrees: a semi-authority position I must neither abuse nor shirk.

Whatever we come up with seems like weak tea, or Chandler's paper cup. I am not sure if she gets my metaphors, since she's looking for a literal life raft, some piece of me to hold onto until next time, anxious before reentering the chaos of home, blah blah blah. When I ask her what she might be feeling when she asks her question, the best she can say is 'nervous.' About what? 'About whether I'll make it. What do you think? You're the expert.'

It is precisely here that the Bogie cynicism and sunny optimism are at odds, in a no man's land. Received analytic wisdom says, 'keep at it, stay curious, maybe in half a century you'll get somewhere.' Yet the other voice strangely carries more heft and gravitas, the dampened trench coat sticking to the shoulders, nearly comforting. *Forget it, Doc, it's antidote-town.*

Wait, stay with the feelings.

Feelings shmeelings! Hit the snooze button, pop a Xanny, switch on Netflix, back to la la land! Hell's bells, let her babble, then smile and nod and give her the bumper sticker at the end, 'sure she'll make it, uh-huh, everything's jake,' and will that be cash or check?

Linda was full fee. Was I afraid to rock the boat for that reason?

Maybe I too like the shortcut. *Ya don't say*. So that's it then, take the money and run?

I shudder at such cravenness. And yet ...

I make notes about the case for a possible paper. It is here in the meta-phorical darkroom that a different picture develops, more fusion than binary, where the divisively gnawing feeling becomes a strange sort of asset ...

This subjective tugging, like a torn hamstring, reminds me of my own chaotically volatile childhood home, where there was laughter one minute, raging tears the next, and back again. Impossible to predict the next emotional earthquake. That turnabout was maddening and reminiscent of Linda's rapid oscillation.

My childhood home was messy, disordered.... I was ashamed to have friends over. This place is a wreck, a grade-school friend once joked, and that was it. No more invites.

I kept that world hidden, amplifying shame. Walking through my front door was like entering a black hole. Boundaries were both rigid and non-existent; in wintertime, the freezing air seeped through the cracks in the doors and windows. Yet jacking the radiators made it unbearably hot. This sums it up.

You never knew what was for dinner, if parents would be home before bedtime. I caught an allergy to chaos, as it was everyone for themselves. 'Five strangers who share a house,' a few therapists remarked.

Eighth grade: things got really bad. Picked on at school, which I kept to myself, as parents were too preoccupied with their flaming Hindenburg of a marriage. Anxious evenings under the blanket, listening to them storm at each other at midnight, Athena and Zeus hurling thunderbolts, a cage fight. A vacuum of dread, that torn-ness—like Linda's yes or no, gnawing away.

Fortunately, I had my siblings, my sister especially, who was Laurel to my Hardy, Costello to my Abbot.

My love of noir also begins here; I loved to quote the Bogie lines to her, which made her laugh: rich and deep, like music. I can still hear it.

It probably started with Bugs Bunny, who parodied gangsters and forties films. We quoted Bugs, who quoted Cagney. This leavened my family's crazed, mind-twisting antics. We would say to my father, passed out on the couch or floor: 'Hey Dad, one more case for the road?' Or: 'Um ... tired?!'

As Linda jokes about celebrities and their pompousness, my sister and I made fun of my dad's malapropisms, slurred pronunciations, a rebellion against the addictive tyranny that was eating us alive. Zeus was out of control, hurling verbal daggers at all who protested.

Thus, the bittersweet nature of such memories, considering the tragedy that followed. Linda's endearing laughter is superimposed upon her own background of doom. This accounts for my dread. My patient (a symbolic sibling in my care) is courting catastrophe if things don't change, joking with the house on fire. (And my dad once fell asleep in bed with a cigarette. Mom said, 'He woke up just in time. Too bad.')

In other words, my childhood home was like Linda's; she reports feeling like an only child, as I often did as the oldest, a little psychotherapist (Atwood, 2015), as Linda had to accommodate her mother's demands and father's erratic to and fro.

I sense Linda prereflectively emulates the either/or of her early organization when she springs her question on me. This jars associations.

I jot down memories of my father for the first time in many years, as if inviting my adult self back into the shameful wreckage of my childhood living room. It's a squeamishness I sense from patients too, who blame themselves for their own neglect. But clinical necessity demands it! Like patients, I dodge pain until it's time to drink from the bitter cup.

My father often held me hostage after dinnertime (if there was dinner), starting in grade school, when I wanted to play or watch my shows, him grilling me about what I was learning, what my 'stupid' teachers were leaving out. Much of his instruction centered around social injustice (he was a social worker [sic]). Some of it was interesting, most of it wasn't.

He might ask about current events, imperative I be 'well informed,' martini in hand. (I would later copy this habit faithfully.) The incongruity is comical and tragic—noir'ish.

As I write about this, I see that here is where a requirement for sainthood begins, a coerced setting aside of nearly all my own needs, wants, and impulses (the early start of my analytic candidacy). To do otherwise was to risk searing shame or rage at my 'exaggerating' the chaos and misery I witnessed, their sharp-edged deflection. School, including books and creative writing, became a refuge … then and now.

It was my father's insistence on his children's attunement to his needs that led to an unrecognized abandonment and unbearable loneliness. In fact all three of his children, myself included, wrestled in adulthood with addictive demons of their own.

I managed miraculously to get sober from drugs and alcohol in my early thirties. (Gruelingly difficult.) My sister went in and out of recovery, overdosing ten years ago, on Halloween, at the young age of 42, only a few years after my father died. I do not think this a coincidence.

I recall our inside jokes. I wonder what she would say about COVID, of Trump … of the niece (my daughter), whom she will never meet. They share a similar sense of humor. Like Linda's, come to think of it.

I am grateful for my sister, in that I was not completely alone in witnessing the awful savagery of alcoholism, shredding any graciousness or warmth between my parents, replacing it with a near-feral contempt, even hatred.

I was not crazy. She saw it too! But then the demons consumed her.

When her own drinking escalated alarmingly, in her twenties, her laughter became more hollow or even manic: more joking with the house on fire. As I often feel with Linda, who was borderline suicidal seemingly yesterday, now prattling on about who's divorcing whom. 'And what's the deal with Kanye?'

I know I cannot rush the process, we are doing the best we can. *And you're happy to collect the dough, aren't ya Doc?*

It dawns on me through writing that the divisiveness, the 'yes/no' dilemma of the doorknob question, is what paralyzes, since the question itself is repetitively transferential for me, and impossibly difficult for Linda. She becomes a kind of caregiver figure for me: a paternal demanding from me with the either/or of compliance, the stultifying nightly ritual. It was too dangerous to disappoint him, and I fear doing so now in the consulting room.

In exploring the work we are doing, on the page and in private, I look at our interaction from different angles. Anxiety drains my energy, freezes mobility. When she 'pops the question' to me, the mood becomes fraught. Thus, a repetitive anxiousness at not being able to answer a question that surely plagues her too. Will she make it, yes or no? But the entire system is toxic.

The need for me to come down on the either/or is also emblematic of her dilemma: she too is right or wrong, good or bad. Her humor about television, meanwhile, reminds me of a young girl playing with a friend. I feel a bit used, unwittingly, my subjectivity shackled—as she must have felt throughout her entire existence. When such process is coenacted rather than explored in the patient's concretizing universe, one feels like cheap goods. Perhaps both of us are trapped in a noir, where a coverup has prevailed for too long.

Mirror, Mirror

Another session, another delving into pop culture, followed by the microdetails of her daughter's treatment. The shadowed rows on the wall. From one angle they look like railroad tracks. From another, prison bars.

Linda arrived late today, after waiting in line at the pharmacy to pick up her daughter's medication. Her daughter is sleeping, though if she runs out of medication, there's risk of relapse. Better safe than sorry, again at Linda's expense. I ask her about this, and she launches into a series of questions about whether or not she should trust her daughter. Is she really passing those urine tests or faking it? Is her therapist holding her feet to the fire?

Linda says, 'I'm sure she's lying her ass off.' She takes a breath

I suddenly say, 'So, think she's gonna make it?'

Linda laughs. 'Hey, that's my question!'

'Just getting a head start.'

She hesitates. 'I'm really not supposed to ask you that, am I?' She looks embarrassed.

I say yes, she's allowed to ask! Why wouldn't she, given how much she loves her daughter, and how scary all this is? I wonder aloud if I've ever really answered her.

'Maybe no one can,' she says glumly.

'Which leaves you in such a dilemma.'

After a moment she talks about her worry, her deep fear that she could lose her daughter—unimaginable terror. As a father, this grips me too, as Linda becomes a kind of daughter I fear abandoning, as I myself was abandoned. We are in a way asymmetrically mourning a lost childhood. Her father left the family when she was in grade school, and died in poor health five years ago. This potential loss is likely more catastrophic than she has let on. She wishes to be 'good' in not repeating archaic patterns with her child, wanting to live in a foreign country without knowing the language. This leads to more inadequacy, like a character from Kafka: guilty of an unspecified crime.

Linda surprises me by saying she knows she should back off, that her kid should be in a sober living, as others have suggested, but she just can't kick her out.

'Scary to think of her out there on her own,' I say.

'But it's not great with her at home, either.' She again complains about the mess, the smart-alecky posts on Instagram. 'I'm tired of cleanin' up her shit!' she says.

Then she looks pensive, perhaps ready to ask 'the question.' She senses I sense it.

Her face flushes crimson. 'That question really puts you on the spot.'

It suddenly occurs to me that she protects *me* with the doorknob question, as if a quick yes or no detours an agony long seen as threatening to *others*. In a way it protects our relationship, which she fears losing. Antidotal, yes, but this is how her world has been jerry-rigged.

It strikes me that she must feel tremendous shame in my witnessing her parenting 'catastrophe,' as she deems it: shame in inviting others into her home. (I can relate!) Her pleasant chatting about pop culture is not, as I initially imagined it, only for her, but also for me in not being 'a difficult' or 'demanding' patient.

Maybe 'is she gonna be ok' camouflages a deeper question such as, 'Am I ok now, in your eyes? Am I screwed up beyond repair?'

Again, the analogues are striking, in that she too is, and always was compelled to be, a little psychotherapist of sorts, under penalty of violence; no one has ever given her permission to even ask for help, as if even needing help was 'wrong.' Perhaps this is behind the ambivalence I sensed from the beginning: 'Fix this and send me home!'

I tell her that I cannot imagine anything more important than her feelings and concerns for her child's safety. But addiction is ruthless, taking families hostage; there are things we can work on to help her out of this jam, relieve pressure to 'fix' things that are out of her control.

'Which is the pressure your parents piled on, isn't it,' I say, 'as if here again you're so fucking responsible. That must be … whew.'

After a few long moments of staring at the shadows, Linda quietly says, 'It never ends.' She discusses her husband's ruthless criticisms, adding, 'I mean he may as well just get a gun and shoot me.'

'But you'd have to go out and buy the gun,' I say.

'And the bullets, probably,' she says, a grim laugh. She leans back wearily into the couch, as if cradled in soft arms.

I say a moment later, 'There's never room for you.'

'Never,' she says, with a determination I have not yet heard. It is her acknowledging such despair, unerringly, that for the first time gives me hope.

The kind of dark humor at play here elasticized our clinical rigidity, allowing a bit of transitional space (Winnicott, 1971) or breathing room for the patient's sadness, anger, and desire to live more freely, at least in the clinical hours. My encouragement disconfirmed that her affectivity was 'burdensome' to me: a chance for her to breathe and get out from under the rock of ceaseless, crushing expectation. Noir'ish humor helped our cause.

It also loosened the temporal trap of an ever-expanding, repetitive sameness, the infinitizing of the present. With even just a bit of fresh air, a 20-year analysis suddenly didn't seem so long.

Say It Again, Sam

Writing about this case and others like it has helped me see that what is truly noir'ish is the patient's traumatizing context(s), the suffocatingly fraught mood of such environments bleeding into the consulting room: crimes without recognition, unnoticed—leading to the coverup and corruption of the child's perceptions, an epistemological homicide.

For the child (or adult) this is terrifying to acknowledge, as it implicates caregivers in unsettling ways, as patients discover this was the farthest thing from love. The answer to Linda's question was no, she is not okay, 'she' meaning the abandoned child taking on the world. Until she and I began to explore that catastrophe, it was impossible for her to state she needed help with her daughter—which I was fortunately able to provide, as I am savvy about addiction (alas).

Let us think for a moment of the (often misogynistic) femme fatale of classic noir: a woman likely traumatized or abused, which the older movies only allude to, now compelled to enact rather than understand her childhood abuse, which terrifies even herself. ('I'm bad, baby,' such women often say to the man they are about to destroy.) In my own practice such unseen abuse includes the intergenerational ravages of addiction, with enslavement and demands on children—and later adults—who become either addicted or beholden to serving addicted others.

This was the elephant I somehow could not address with Linda, as I was only just discovering it in my own history. It was painful, and often hard to stomach.

Until then our enactment unfolded in the venetian shadows of my consulting room. I first had to solve my own 'case,' at least grieve the 'corpse' of murdered innocence. It seemed that Linda, via her last minute yes-or-no, 'put the squeeze on me,' as Bogie might say: 'Put up or shut up.'

But writing about it helped draw the chalk around our parallel abandonments, showing how strongly both of us had wounds that were scabbed over, unrecognized, paralyzing analytic mobility. This led to a frustration and fear that Linda was holding me back, that I was possibly inadequate, as if I could 'fix' what could not be fixed, just as I fleetingly wondered as a child if dad's drinking was a reflection on my own worthiness, and what I could do to mitigate it. In some ways I am still waiting for the 'Godot' (Beckett, 1954) of his validation, never to arrive.

I subsequently, gingerly confirmed how Linda actually minimized the burden on me, rather than pursue the unthinkable expression of her own long-dissociated desires, guidance, and protection, which she could only imagine as shamefully overwhelming the other and jeopardizing attachment. My hesitation to answer her must have reinforced all this.

One could say that she was, per Brandchaft (2010), maintaining ties to constrictive family ideology. She was a femme fatale in that sense, pointing the weapon at herself.

To loosen proceedings, I had to recognize and grieve my losses, realize I was not completely 'past it,' allowing some raw sadness to emerge via writing that brought ventilation ... to that soulful ache of loss, with a sister who could not survive her own addiction, as acknowledging her own pain was incriminating to caregivers she had been brainwashed to protect. Addictive systems are themselves the raw stuff of noir.

What is ironic too is that I hesitated to join Linda's playfulness, her laughter, because it was tempting, as if I might enjoy it 'too much,' sidetracking the serious work. Understanding such hesitation was an aspect the work.

It is hard in writing all this to overlook the irony of becoming an analyst in the first place, specializing in addiction no less, wherein any success can never 'undo' catastrophic losses.

Couldn't save your sis, eh Doc? Shame ...

Such a synthesis, hopeful and tragic both, is often discovered in analytic writing—including the composition of this very chapter—a kind of joyous heartbreak, expanding awareness I then take with me into the work. The work dialogues with the creative process as such process also influences the treatment.

For our analytic writing, like the dyad itself, illuminates unseen existential suffering, unthinkable tragedies. Like the analytic relationship also, which for all of the depth of connection and soulful overlap, is prompted by the trauma and catastrophe that brings patients to our office—and the analyst to her chair, in hope of investigation, meaning, and some measure of redemption. This we do collaboratively, a way of saying (to paraphrase Bogie one last time), *Patient, I think this is the beginning of a beautiful twinship ...*

References

Atwood, G.E. (2011). *The abyss of madness.* New York: Routledge.

Atwood, G.E. (2015). Credo and reflections. *Psychoanalytic Dialogues,* 25: 137–152.

Beckett, S. (1954). *Waiting for Godot.* New York: Grove Atlantic.

Brandchaft, B. (2010). Systems of pathological accommodation in psychoanalysis. In B. Brandchaft, S. Doctors, & D. Sorter, *Toward an emancipatory psychoanalysis: Brandchaft's intersubjective vision* (pp. 193–220). New York: Routledge.

Chandler, R. (n.d.). Retrieved December 4, 2020, from https://libquotes.com/raymond-chandler/quote/lbr1r3x.

Miller, A. (1981). *The drama of the gifted child.* New York: Basic Books.

Polanski, R. (Director) (1974). *Chinatown* [film]. Paramount Pictures.

Shengold, L. (1989). *Soul murder: The effects of childhood abuse and deprivation.* New Haven, CT: Yale University Press.

Winnicott, D.W. (1971). *Playing and reality.* Oxon, UK: Routledge.

Chapter 3

Intimate Strangers

Albert Camus and Absurdity in Psychoanalysis

Introduction

I struggled with how to respond to a patient calling me stupid.

After a few months of treatment, my keenly intelligent patient, Patricia, was becoming irritable—provoked by my asking about her feelings, in the midst of our increasingly concretized interaction. My confusion deepened when I inquired about her irritation. 'You're not answering me,' she might say, curtly, as if standing at a customer service window.

My patient was nicknamed 'Tish,' her pronunciation as a toddler, which her parents found endearing; one of the only things, it seemed. Her mother, a litigation attorney, had been scorchingly critical, especially when Tish dared to voice any hurt feelings. Meanwhile Tish's mild-mannered, professorial father remained unengaged and often drunk.

Tish came to me in hopes of 'getting over my traumas' (sic), and receiving guidance in exiting a relationship with an alcoholic, verbally abusive boy-friend. Her feelings oscillated from rage to shame and self-criticism, for being too harsh or not harsh enough to end 'another failed relationship.' She was keen to learn about recovery for partners of alcoholics, a specialty of mine.

Tish arrived just after I left my job as a rehab counselor and entered private practice; while I remained well-versed in recovery concepts, I longed to expand into the kind of analytic work I studied at my institute. I was especially taken with intersubjective-systems theory, particularly the work of Brandchaft (2010) on pathological accommodation, a concept which meshed with my desire, and patients,' for freedom from centralized affective constriction.

My hopes were high, my knowledge of recovery sound, and what was theoretically required seemed straightforward enough: engage with the patient in a conjoined empathic exploration of binding, prereflective 'killer' organizing principles (Stolorow, 1999). I expected it all to proceed as smoothly as a Beethoven sonata.

So why such difficulty? We had an engaged and friendly rapport, appreciated each other's humor, and our sessions seemed productive. She

DOI: 10.4324/9781003266358-4

mentioned occasionally that therapy helped her set 'stronger boundaries.' Tish was an excellent student (and a schoolteacher) and learned quickly, in a process we both seemed to enjoy. It all appeared a bit superficial at moments, but who was I to judge? Best to avoid falling into a hermeneutics of suspicion (Orange, 2011).

One day Tish announced she wanted to attend her first recovery meeting, to find the courage to finally leave her boyfriend.

Except my 'explanation' of recovery fell flat. An edge of frustration crept in, as she stated I was failing to explain *why* the meeting might help, or *how* the twelve steps led to freedom? I sensed trouble in paradise.

I hoped recovery would assist our process (since she came but once a week), to help her cope with her often tumultuous feelings between sessions. But inquiring after such affect only agitated her further, and I became a bit confused.

Tish stated her feelings had been relayed at the outset of treatment; why did she need to repeat them again? She now needed a thorough 'explanation' of recovery, very slow in coming.

The atmosphere thickened.

I said something like, 'well recovery like therapy is more "experiential" than conceptual.' 'Fine,' she responded, 'explain "experiential".'

Silence.

I felt possessed by an odd wordlessness, while inwardly bristling at her implied demands. She rebuffed, it appeared, the empathic inquiry advised by my chosen theory—which also cautioned against 'blaming the patient.' How, then, to understand this?

My uncertainty and hesitation increased Tish's anxiety. At one point she stated it was I who initially suggested she attend meetings, which confused me further. (I did?) I *did* recall she had 'bolted' from her last therapist after nine months, finding him inadequately versed in recovery. I feared becoming another abandoning male caregiver.

Once or twice she commented that my questions about her feelings were 'stupid.' Her comment stung, but in supervision I had been encouraged to think of such responses as self-protection, rather than oppositional or 'defensive.' I got the message; our patients are not here to protect us.

I tried this: 'I'm sensing here you want or *need* answers, unlike your last therapist, like maybe there's anxiety about being let down again.'

'Yes,' she said drily. Then, silence.

I said, 'So I imagine you're feeling ... disappointed?'

Tish replied, 'Well, *duh*.'

A long pause.

Why was I having such difficulty with Tish? The atmosphere had become vaguely alienating ... void-like. Would this therapy, too, go under? Or was this fear a sign of my own insecurity? Empathic understanding remained stubbornly 'unformulated' (Stern, 2003). Mostly I felt estranged from the tranquil worldhood I thought we had established. (*We're pals, ain't we?*)

Comments about my 'stupid' question appeared almost menacing, in contrast to the promise of early days, as the patient's appreciative mask fell away to reveal a stranger ... a vaguely threatening one at that.

Under the Rock

This vignette serves as an analytic example of what the writer Albert Camus (1913–1960) referred to as 'absurdity,' our human encounter with what Ben and Robert Stolorow (2011) call the 'absurdity of our finite, mortal existence.' This often-eerie encounter with a kind of void can result in alienation or estrangement, cutting against the grain of habituated perceptions. In the case above, it was as if the patient had become a stranger to me—and I to her, mutually undermining assumptions. My own beloved theory meanwhile became less inspiring and more a set of 'rules' I was failing.

In this chapter I will illustrate how Camus' concepts and metaphors have been helpful in understanding such quicksands, in ways that also parallel Stolorow's (2007) descriptions of traumatic encounters with finitude and death anxiety, which can impact our very going-on-being (Winnicott, 1965).

What is absurdity for Camus? His book *The Myth of Sisyphus* (1942/1983), written in tandem with his still-controversial novel *The Stranger* (1942/1988), presents a philosophical meditation on this theme. The book is not a formal philosophical position, rather more of a lyrical essay on the dilemma of facing vast unknowns. Camus describes the paradox of a future that contains the possible fulfillment of our deepest yearnings ... and our own demise, at a date to be determined.

Absurdity here is the tension between our yearning for a soothingly continuous rational or expectable world-experience, and the inevitable, alienating upending of such hopes or expectations. Camus saw the world as mostly indifferent to the latter. (I will, later in this chapter, outline ways in which this perspective of 'the world' is in part derived from Camus' own psychobiography (Atwood & Stolorow, 1993).)

Camus begins *Sisyphus* by depicting absurdity as a sense of uncanniness— what Stolorow (2015), in discussing Heidegger, calls a feeling of 'not-at-homeness.' In such moments, our usual habit of living or perceiving, our tranquilizing 'absolutisms' (Stolorow, 2007) of imagined permanence, are pierced; an unexpected illness, injury, or loss (or political outcome), witnessing any manner of shocking social injustices, all undermine certainties we may not even be aware of until they are shaken. The world is suddenly organized or (dis)ordered in unexpectedly jarring ways.

At such moments, Camus states, in his lyrical and occasionally abstract style, our universe is 'suddenly divested of illusions and lights, man feels an alien, a stranger.... This ... is properly the feeling of absurdity' (1942/1983, p. 6). Our Sisyphean attempts to make a 'home,' in a world that stubbornly resists such home-making, are continually undermined, in ways we cannot always predict. We are forced to wrestle with an absurdity that is constitutive of human experiencing, as 'absurdity depends as much on man as on the world.... It is all that links them together' (p. 21).

Like intersubjective-systems theorists, Camus eschews Cartesianism, or any falsely supreme rationality or metaphysics, since 'that universal reason, practical or ethical, that determinism, those categories that explain everything are enough to make a decent man laugh' (pp. 20–21). Camus believed such alienation had become endemic to the modern person, divested of the comforts of mass religion or faith in institutions, even rationality itself: a world capricious, unjust, even violent. *Sisyphus*, after all, was written during the Nazi takeover of Europe.

Camus begins the book by speaking of suicide, asking if life is worth living, and if so why, or how—but his true interest lies in exploring the enlivening pursuit of personalized meaning, while cautioning against an escape into numbing habit or existential aversion. He recognizes the paradoxical conflict between our personalized hopes of fulfillment and life's absurdly jarring contingencies; such unwelcome tremors or 'earthquakes' (to say nothing of finitude itself) can threaten the ensured consistency or reliable survival of what or who we value. Beloved others, for instance, are like ourselves mortal, meaning love is so often overshadowed by loss. Similarly, we experience encounters with others (including clinically) when values we privilege (or possibly the relationship itself) appear threatened—as with Tish, above, who seemed to devalue empathic exploration.

How to stay purposeful and engaged, Camus wonders, without lapsing into a waking sleep, a disengaged cynicism or reflexive nihilism? This human endeavor can appear impossible at times—Sisyphean, like dyadic processing in difficult moments. 'The world has become ... an unknown landscape where my heart can lean on nothing,' he wrote (1963/2010, p. 170).

Camus wrote *Sisyphus* in his late twenties, influenced by Kierkegaard, Nietzsche, and Heidegger, whose *Being and Time* (1927/1962) was beginning to revolutionize western philosophy. Camus discusses the 'climate' of Heidegger's thought, specifically our existential anxiety in Being-toward-death, where 'the world can no longer offer anything to the man filled with anguish' (Heidegger, quoted in Camus, 1942/1983, p. 23). Camus urges, like Heidegger, that we reject the tempting distractions of 'Das Man,' the mainstream 'chatter' that averts or numbs us from the search for individualized purpose, anything that becomes a cocoon. This might apply, in the analytic context, to any narcotizingly inflexible theory or position.

Camus was also informed by existentialist literature, especially Dostoevsky and Kafka, as well as classical Greek philosophy and mythology—including *Sisyphus'* eponymous figure, doomed by Zeus to roll his boulder at the top of a mountain. Here was a mythically absurd and unspeakable 'penalty in which the whole being is exerted toward accomplishing nothing' (p. 130). (Those who work with addicted patients or couples may relate.)

One of the themes of Camus' book is that we are always already situated toward such nothingness, as our embeddedness in time leads inexorably towards the most terrifying unknown of all: our own demise (and, I would add, the demise of those we love). *Our* death is an experience we cannot actually reflect upon since 'in reality there is no experience of death … it is barely possible to speak of others' deaths. It is a substitute, an illusion, and it never quite convinces us' (pp. 14–15). Death, he says, becomes 'the supreme abuse' (p. 90).

Thus we face the difficult human task of finding a way to live with purpose, while a Damoclean expiration date hangs over all of us.

Camus speaks of the mythical Sisyphus as a mortal whose hatred of this 'abuse,' together with his passion for life (and rebellion against authoritarian gods) leads to his eternal fate. Such fate carries a sense of cosmic injustice, endured by a humankind repetitively abandoned or betrayed by omnipotent overseers. (Camus' personal experience reflects such an abandonment; in infancy he lost his father.)

Camus states that absurdity leads him to rely on three guiding principles: rebellion, freedom and passion—while keeping one's own human limitations in mind. (Camus was ever wary of absolutes.)

There is of course a fine tradition of rebellion in psychoanalysis, leading to the establishment of new theories, perspectives, even institutes. Camus, like intersubjective-systems theorists, emphasized liberation from tyrannical thought-systems; in *Sisyphus* he develops a humanly-grounded rebellion against finitude's obscuring shadow, in finding one's distinctive self-expression, and 'overcoming [a person's] phantoms and approaching a little closer his naked reality' (p. 115).

Sisyphus' fateful repetition thus resembles our own alienating deflation or thwarted expectations, leading perhaps to traumatic portkeys (Stolorow, 2007) or feeling-states. Camus states that Sisyphus, in spite of his fate, retains the freedom to uncover meaning in his task besides torment and futility. In fact, Camus states at the book's conclusion that 'we must imagine Sisyphus happy' (1942/1983, p. 123), in resisting the foreclosure of authentic possibilities.

Camus' own childhood, in French-occupied Algeria, came with a require-ment to loyally protect an impoverished, uneducated family—of which, he only later admitted, he was deeply ashamed. Traumatic finitude came early, when his father Lucien died in World War I while Camus was an infant. Such an unspeakable loss, shadowing his entire life and work (combined with his family's impoverishment, in a colonized world consisting of native Algerians understandably resentful towards the French), instilled from the outset an almost foundational alienation. This is to say nothing of Camus' abusive grandmother, who ran the house, and his numbed, distant mother. Fair to say that the young Camus lived in a no-person's-land.

Camus, like the intersubjective theorists referred to earlier, remained attuned to the significance of *lived* affectivity: 'Like great works, deep feelings always mean more than they are conscious of saying' (p. 10). There are parallels between the concept of personalized worldhoods (Stolorow, Atwood & Orange, 2002) and Camus' observation that

> Great feelings take with them their own universe ... light up with their passion an exclusive world.... There is a universe of ambition, of selfishness.... What is true of ... specialized feelings will be even more so of emotions ... aroused by absurdity.
>
> (1942/1983, pp. 9–10)

It is Camus' descriptions of the affectively absurd that, for this analyst, help give voice to a variety of void-like clinical 'crunches,' including awkward clinical moments, moments of estrangement from patients, or even my own theory—when the grounding guidance of mentors strangely becomes 'nothing but contradictions and nonsense' (Camus, 1942/1983, p. 27). Moments, in other words, when aspirations or developmental hopes are threatened, in ways both unexpected and familiar, as if one or both participants are 'portkey'd' to eternal entrapment in isolating frustration, without reprieve.

Such repetitive experiencing might, for an analyst, appear as a threat to the analytic relationship, as was the case above with Tish—with potentially dire implications for her well-being, my own empathic skills, a new practice, and so on (fears rooted mostly in prereflective trauma of my own), should I somehow 'fail her.'

Stolorow (2015) describes moments when absurdity or startling reminders of our mortal vulnerability rob us of 'the tranquilizing illusions of the everyday world.... [When] the fundamental defensive purpose ... of average everydayness has failed' (p. 131). This is but one reason Camus says our narcotizing cocoons (or fast-held ideas) will not work, *even as we cannot help seeking them*. Like Sisyphus, we resist acknowledging our finitude. At the same time, any 'victory' of transcending finitude is 'the one I shall never have' (Camus, 1942/1983, p. 87).

Yet Camus maintains an optimism (tinged with irony), emphasizing continued activity or creativity, *lived* experience, rather than the *cordon sanitaire* of protective concepts or ideologies. Of course, we may not realize we are clinging to such concepts until relational absurdities reveal them to us. In fact, such existential fallibility can bind us in analogic or communal yearning: 'In this vulnerable universe everything that is human and solely human assumes a more vivid meaning.... These are the true riches because they are transitory' (p. 88).

***

Like Camus, Brandchaft (2010) encourages an empathic rebellion against authoritative dictates from archaic systems, towards 'risky' authenticity. Both he and Camus employ the prison cell as a metaphor for existential confinement. Both also observe the grueling diligence required for emancipation, as systems that imprison also *protect*—an absurdity in itself, and profoundly challenging for analytic process.

Still, Brandchaft recognizes the sanctity of a person's distinctive selfhood. Doctors (2017), in a recent and helpful overview, states that Brandchaft passionately advocated analysts' struggling on behalf of patients' unique self-reflective processes and point of view. This echoes Camus' exhortations to struggle for one's own distinctive authenticity.

Though here again absurdity lurks: it took Camus decades to write about his own early emotional devastations, given impossible archaic demands to protect a family of which he was simultaneously ashamed. Similarly, an analyst may find herself ensnared in enmeshing transferential ties (including to theories or supervisors), while yearning to find her own clinical voice.

Clinical absurdity might also include the surprising, asymmetrical provocation of disavowed trauma, instances where patients' developmental segregations begin to unwittingly dovetail with unseen accommodations of the analyst. At the time, of course, it can appear that the patient is simply 'refusing to cooperate' with our heartfelt agenda.

There is also absurdity in the notion of providing an analytic emancipation of uncertain duration or cost to patients, which often provokes the terror of dependence or types of enmeshments (Brandchaft, 1991) that some patients have long averted. This is to say nothing of inevitable analytic 'failures' that retraumatize, leaving Ferenczian (1932) blood on the analyst's hands, unwittingly repeating the 'act of murder previously perpetuated against the patient' (p. 58).

One begins to sense the importance of analysts' own empathic support. Camus, in fact, stresses the value of camaraderie and *fraternité*—due not only to cherished democratic ideals, but also protracted seclusions in quarantine, as well as the suffocating emotional aridity of his childhood.

***

In his teens Camus contracted tuberculosis, in those days tantamount to a death sentence. He survived, though it put an end to his hopes of a career in soccer, at which he excelled; a loss he regretted the rest of life (Lottman, 1997). His doctors often prescribed time in the mountains for long, isolated periods. This may be one reason he cherished the communal vitality of both soccer and the theater, an enlivenment also sought via political activism and journalism. The support of paternal mentors, too, was crucial to his creative process; Camus, after all, wanted to outline the void, since the 'absurd creator … must give the void its colors' (1942/1983, p. 113).

Such voids might become foregrounded, in dyadic situations, via the asymmetrical collapse of participants' hopes. Patients might begin to feel the echoes of isolation, even disillusionment, when it dawns on them that rather than 'deleting' the dangerous trauma-affect they have necessarily segregated, the analyst will in fact be leading them *directly* into that den of beasts.

(While charging a fee!) Here we sense incommensurable worldhoods (Stolorow & Schwartz, 2002), a clash of meaning-systems, where what is terrifying for a patient is of near-sacred importance for the analyst. How each participant defines what therapy even *is* can be incommensurable at the start, as if absurdity is there waiting for us.

This can provoke repetitive anxiety for analysts who were subject to what Atwood (2015) calls the scenario of 'the little psychotherapist,' a child enlisted early to 'support and sustain a depressed or otherwise emotionally troubled parent' (p. 150). Atwood cites Alice Miller's (1979) description of the 'gifted child,' an imprisonment involving 'the dissociation of … the child's personality as the child is not allowed to become the person he or she might have been' (Atwood, 2015, p. 150). Here we have the absurdity of the *child's* subjectivity becoming 'toxic' in a noxious system. (Again, we find parallels here with marginalized communities, whose mere presence becomes grounds for existential oppression.)

This, for our present purposes, becomes the quintessential relational absurdity: that of an overburdened child (Brandchaft, 2010) struggling to 'manage' or regulate the subjectivities of others, even an entire system, as her own developmental selfhood is buried beneath an avalanche of demands. When this traumatic experience 'repeats' in analysis (likely inevitable), relatedness becomes undermined, as one or both participants fear or dread disappointing the other, revealing 'shameful' subjective inadequacies.

In fact, Camus himself was a gifted child, whose ongoing accommodation of his withdrawn, silent mother held dire implications for a lifetime of relational frustration and despair. Camus, in an early journal entry, states that 'the strange feeling which the son has for his mother constitutes his whole sensibility,' adding that 'whoever notices this himself feels … a guilty conscience' (both 1963/2010, p. 3); such guilt hints at the danger of yearning for a worldhood *of one's own*—which 'abandons' the wounded caregiver. Meanwhile, Camus' biographer describes long, deadening afternoons in which Camus did nothing but observe his mother staring dolefully into the street (Lottman, 1997).

Sisyphus' metaphors illuminate such experiences, moments when we bump up against apparently asphyxiating demands for accommodation—including dyadically, when alienating silences or uncertainties seem to undermine participants' hopes.

The way in which Camus gives language to such experiences inspires my own clinical creativity (Orange, 2010) at such moments, to lean in rather than circumvent them—much as we are asking patients to do. Such 'leaning in' often, of course, yields a necessary yet painful re-alignment (Brandchaft, 1994) or 'stretched' reflectivity. Such struggle also, hopefully, provides a window into the *patient's* unspeakable agonies, the glimmer of a shared twinship-in-absurdity, yet unborn.

I'm with Stupid

In the case of Tish, a spontaneous moment led to a breakthrough.

One particular session darkened with yet another discussion of recovery concepts; she had attended a meeting and was dissatisfied, since attending had been *my* idea.

Her questions had me tongue tied. What was I missing here? How to move us to a more open-ended exploration? I felt I was flailing, started to actually feel a bit … stupid.

I simply could not find a way around her self-protective wall. I felt handcuffed in needing to stay distant while deeply attuned. Yet I was the expert; it said so on my website.

I smiled patiently and said, 'So … let's talk about what you might be feeling about all this.'

A scowl. 'Come on, that's a stupid question.'

I winced. (This was new.)

Had I slipped up? Then, I noticed … on her face … not a scowl, but concern: genuine, vaguely anxious, as if the mask (as I perceived it) of lurking hostility had slipped, much as my own 'professionalism' slipped when I winced.

Something cleared, like the sweeping of leaves from a windshield, and I said, 'My God … this is really scary for you.'

She nodded.

'You're so afraid about being let down *again*.' I *felt* it now, as a genuinely dreadful outcome she lived with, *all the time*. 'I probably could've said it better, but … remember the "little girl" we talked about?' She nodded again. 'Well, I want to hear what *she* has to say, so *all* of you is welcome here.'

'Thank you,' she said, and burst into tears.

A few moments later she said, still crying, 'I'm so tired of doing this all by myself.'

'So lonely,' I said.

Then we were a few minutes over. She stood and said, 'My comment about the questions being stupid … did that bother you?'

I hesitated. 'Well, it's not my *favorite* thing.'

She laughed and said, 'Fair enough.'

I added, 'Though I think it makes me want to back off a bit.'

'Gotcha,' she said, flashing me an 'a-ok' sign on her way out the door.

***

The empathic, Camusian 'rebellion' on my part here was not only the wince, but the sustained curiosity that followed, rather than a collapse into defensiveness or anxious retreat. Thankfully, Tish joined me in this newly-opened space. Her worried reaction to my wince disconfirmed the fear that she was the 'demanding' stranger I dreaded, which in turn showed *her* she was not 'too much' for me, that in fact I wanted to understand her better.

Impressively courageous was her expression of long-dissociated grief. In milieus as aggressively Cartesian as hers had been, moves toward authenticity were practically fatal. In the current context, her inherited self-protections, the fraught 'make or break' quality they introduced (dovetailing with anxieties of my own), were driven by the camouflaged desire for a closer relatedness, and permission to 'be herself.' Vulnerability spontaneously returned, loosening anxious 'grips,' after each of our hopes had become fleetingly, absurdly threatened in parallel yet unformulated fashion.

The intensities of her 'demands,' her sharp-edged questions, were indicative of her archaic worldhood; I experienced them with but a fraction of their original brutality, the thwarting of hopes for safe parental engagement. I became another 'father' who was again failing to protect against, in this case, her critical boyfriend and, perhaps more significantly, her critical 'inner mom.' I also discerned a heartfelt yearning to be guided by a paternal figure, amidst her overwhelm; this was, most likely, why attending meetings became 'my idea,' as her own emotional hunger remained risky even to *acknowledge,* as one sees often in addictive systems.

It's true her wishes for safety manifested as antidotal demands, but this was the 'language' of her early worldhood. Most of my 'difficult' patients, in fact, live in terror of overburdening others. (As did Camus.)

It took me much trial and error to finally attune to my own dread of disappointing *her,* 'failing' to forestall her intolerable grief and anguish, echoing some of my own unseen archaic demands. This paralleled my own early experiences with a father who demanded intellectual mirroring from his young son, to shore up his own shaky selfhood—as the child was not 'dismissed' until he 'got it absolutely right.'

One of the many absurdities of this early little-therapist scenario was not only the rigid silencing of my own self-expression, but the sadness and terror I felt *for him,* as I intuited quite strongly that he was lonely and tortured—a mind-bending role reversal involving a demand that I care for him in the way he prescribed. His 'need' became my own, so that my needs of others (throughout my formative years) began to blur with others' needs *of me,* especially antidotal provision.

With Tish, too, I fought off a dread that my failure to provide her with definitive 'answers' might confirm a crushing and dangerous inadequacy, as if her very survival *depended on* it—a repetitively reinforced concept over many years, unilluminated until not long ago. (In this sense, she was doing me a great favor.)

Such wariness of disappointing an anguished person I cared about only heightened the intensity of an apparent demand for antidotes. Meanwhile, I began postponing the risk of trying to contact her vulnerability, which (I told myself) I would attempt next time, or in the session after that ... soon I would speak up ... to break the silence that imprisoned even as it (somewhat shamefully) protected ... the therapist.

***

When I was seven years old, my father took me to see *The Exorcist* (Blatty & Friedkin, 1973). The film made no sense but naturally scared the hell out of me. The self-mutilation was especially disturbing, including a scene where the possessed girl masturbates violently with a bloody crucifix.

My father told me beforehand that I was 'grown up enough' to view the film, which pleased me to hear, though I felt implicitly I had to act the part.

I had intermittent insomnia for the next couple of years, including a precocious terror of death, which I envisioned as an eternal, isolated abandonment.

I recall that my attempts to relate my terror about all this were met with parental confusion, even derision, since—rationality being dogma—it was 'only a movie,' and death was such a long way off.

What I most recall about the film was the ride home afterward, listening to the suddenly-haunting pop songs on the radio. We did not exchange a word.

***

Camus' estranging childhood left psychic 'fissures' illuminated in part by the marked affective contrasts of *Sisyphus* and *The Stranger*. *Sisyphus* is ironically cheerful, indicative of an idealized self-reliance and the joy of a writer finding his voice. *The Stranger* is darker, its apparent indifference towards society's hypocrisies co-existing with both alienated indifference and a thinly camouflaged, disillusioned rage.

Both books only hint at deeper yearnings and sorrow, made more explicit in his later works, the last of which—his most emotionally transparent—was never finished, due to a fatal car accident. The manuscript for this final novel was found amidst the car's mangled wreckage.

Running in Circles

The email from my patient read, 'Hey D, it's Russ. So holidays not great, wife and daughter moved out. I was drunk, so can't blame her, though she's a nag. Kinda suicidal, but don't worry I'm ok. How was your Christmas?'

Russ was a handsome patient in his mid-thirties, with a lilting southern accent and a polite if halting demeanor, and an ambivalence apparently endemic to his personality.

He initially came to me in summertime to address his drinking, which 'isn't a problem though it is,' for his wife at least. She was 'correct' though she 'should butt out,' he told me.

Russ was a successful software engineer who struggled with Brandchaftian accommodation, at work and especially at home, with a wife who 'monitors me constantly.' He appeared dependent on her for the guidance he loathed, since it reassured the tie, albeit with stringent conditions. He felt both protected and constricted by her monitoring.

It did not take long to see how alcohol served as an antidote to the pain of emotional imprisonment, as developmental hopes remained both 'toxic' (to others) and unavoidable. He could not win for losing, as with the addictive process itself. As Camus observes, there are times when 'not taking what one doesn't desire is the hardest thing in the world' (1942/1983, p. 63).

We developed a friendly and engaged rapport. I found him observant, witty, and hostage to archaic family dictates. His mother had been strictly religious, appointing him the 'day nurse' for his little sister, who suffered from a rare immune disorder which kept her mostly bedridden. Russ' 'nursing' role was described as 'the only decent thing to do ... though I hated it. But, I'm selfish.'

I began to understand the temptation of beer and pot.

Just as we were starting to explore the more underlying affective roots of his 'man-cave ritual,' as he called his drinking, he announced he was taking a break from therapy, 'for the holidays,' due to work-related travel. This was 'nothing personal, we're good.' He announced he was down to one beer a night. His wife was happy, so he was happy, and happy new year.

Shortly thereafter the above email arrived, followed by his sheepish return.

His wife and young daughter were gone, to his great shame (and rage, which he was also ashamed about). They had argued viciously while he was 'shitfaced.' The repressed frustration came flooding out, in an obscenity-laced tirade that frightened her out the door. Soon he was hungover and annihilated by remorse.

He desperately wanted them to return, more willing now to discuss with me the anger he felt at both her and his even more intrusive mother, including the shame he felt at such anger, and the shame about the shame, due to early, non-negotiable prohibitions. Russ acknowledged his mother 'might' have been verbally abusive—humiliating to admit, as he had been expected to not embarrass the family *under any circumstances.*

He also reluctantly related his impatience with his 'wild' toddler, though here I confirmed that, based on personal experience, a young Tasmanian devil could be difficult to supervise. Sparing personal anecdotes about my own parental struggles led to a twinship in parental absurdity. I sensed *he* sensed how much I understood his discovering, in his strong and loving attachment to his daughter, just how much paternal neglect he had experienced, which he strove not to repeat.

He also found it helpful to discuss his achievements, at work and parenting, since so much of his inherent goodness and capability had been historically overlooked.

He did, however, enact ambivalence by occasionally exiting sessions early, or making snarky remarks about my appearance ('ever iron that shirt, dude?') Though he always insisted he was 'really busy' or 'just jokin' respectively.

In spite of these near-constant oscillations, Russ began expressing his hope for familial cohesion, as I got a sense of how infrequently he had seen joy or happiness on the face of an intimate other. His wife and daughter eventually returned home, grateful for a gentler Russ, now attending Alcoholics Anonymous meetings, reluctantly. A mutual fondness grew between us.

Then one day he again reluctantly informed me that he needed to cut back to once a week or every other week. I was caught off guard. He reluctantly stated that he was struggling financially. I agreed to a moderate fee reduction.

This reduction only increased his ambivalence, including a tendency to move quickly away from nearly any affective exploration; we began struggling with drawn-out silences. He began repeating the phrase 'dude, don't read into things too much.' A familiar but nameless dread crept in, like a fog, a vague bewilderment that something was undermining the therapy, 'somehow' related to his elusiveness. Such absurdity-linked *angst* only amplified when he announced, a few weeks later, that he *again* might want to stop treatment—due solely to his production job. I felt irritated—thinking I should not be, this was *my* 'blind spot,' and any protest on my part would be another demand on him.

I said, 'I'm surprised to hear this come up again. Didn't we … just talk about it?'

'Did we?' he said. 'Yeah … no, that was…. Wait, we did … I think?'

I then blurted, pushing aside some internal prohibition, 'I just feel like I have to keep chasing you to do this.'

'Oh,' he said, blushing.

Had I gone too far?

A pause, before he quietly said, 'I have trouble being close to people.'

Then, a most memorable silence … after which, he began to haltingly relate his struggle with relational intimacy, always hitting a barrier *without knowing why,* which 'drives everyone in my life crazy,' further inflaming a tormenting, incomprehensible absurdity *from within his own subjectivity.* This represents one of the cruelest legacies of unacknowledged trauma, as the system absurdly and repeatedly blames 'failure' of emotional regulation squarely on the child—and, later, the agonized adult, who remains impossibly conflicted and ashamed.

The theme of imprisoning affective demands emerged in our discussions, as we discovered that even the hints of others' needs somehow led to entrapment or things he *had* to do to secure the tie (including me, I imagined, though he denied it). Such frustration or 'withdrawal' then led to shame—since the psychological underpinnings eluded him, preventing the articulation of acute anxiety which was always his 'fault.' He was trapped in a psychic cell that was suffocating yet necessary for survival.

I observed that his moves for closer engagement with others led always to non-negotiable demands. 'That's it,' he said, brightening, *'non-negotiable.'* He described the childhood legacy of maintaining or 'managing' fraught attachments which also prohibited relating his hopes or fears, meaning he always had to prioritize others' emotionality: a paradoxical set of 'handcuffs.' Then, feelings about such 'shackling' led to further shame since (as he once said) 'what kind of idiot can't figure out or ask for what he wants?' Thus an anguished ambivalence in which he needed connections which were never safe to need.

At the end of the particular session described above, and with time running out, I said to him that there were two people involved here. I myself had been looking to discuss his original 'cutback,' while hesitating on how to proceed, contributing to the frustration I spontaneously expressed.

He said, 'Well you can't know what's on my mind if I don't tell you.' I countered that I played a part by hesitating, not intruding, possibly like his mother. At this he laughed and said, 'You got nothin' on her.'

'Ok,' I said, 'but if you're struggling ... '

'You're not a mind-reader.'

'Russ—'

'Ok fine you fucked up,' he said. We laughed a few moments ... as I felt grateful he was able to express at least mild disappointment at a caregiver who had backed away, and left him with more than he could handle, as he habitually assumed full responsibility.

***

All of this helped me understand, in an embodied way, the terror of vulnerability lurking throughout Russ' imprisoning self-organizations. His genuine concerns about money and time blended with a habitual, mandated detouring around authentic feeling-states, as dictates of old demanded. These included his prereflectively protecting others from his 'overbearing' strivings, including his distant father—leaving young Russ overwhelmed with self-doubt and unseen abandonment pain. Russ concluded, like so many intelligent, emotionally neglected children, that he was simply too demanding in wanting even a paucity of fatherly guidance and validation.

I suspect my anxious uncertainty and hesitations provoked his fear of becoming 'too much' for me—a fear overlooked when I prereflectively distanced myself from some of my *own* grief regarding profoundly painful paternal abandonments. (This also brings to mind some of Kohut's (1971, 1984) invaluable discussions of instances when analysts must work through their own difficult transferences, to better understand patients' vulnerabilities.)

In this case, an historically reflexive aversion to some of my own abandonment trauma led to misattunements to Russ, and his long-thwarted seeking of validation from an idealized male caregiver. We each, it seemed, had analogous yet unformulated repetitive paternal transferences in play, provoking a vague but menacing dread of 'failing' the other.

There were also, in regard to my own subjective anxiety, the 'demands' of my own theoretical mentors, as described earlier, where inspiring theories became almost absurdly rigid. I had not realized how eager I was to gain approval of *these* symbolic fathers, who I imagined kept an anxious eye out for, like my own father, any sign of 'failure.'

Ironic, since the patient, too, struggled with archaic demands to please or become 'worthy' of his father's attention, by paradoxically 'figuring out' how to not 'need' such shameful guidance or recognition—thus protecting his father. Furtive attempts to 'figure it all out' led to repetitive and ruminative dissociation of the dangerous yearnings he could not completely disavow. It thus remained agonizingly impossible to 'think' his way out of such imprisonment—leading in this case to failing an archaic self-ideal, the demand to save others from his toxic selfhood.

For Russ it was, yet again, his *sole* responsibility to regulate an entire relational context. His pulling back from me in this light becomes a means of self-preservation. We became two closed systems, struggling from within a fraught, mutually-reinforcing shameworld (Orange, 2008).

I initially feared that my comment about 'chasing' him was intrusive or insulting. He disabused me of this, said he felt it as a paternal tap on the shoulder, an underscoring that therapy was important, as was *he* ... to his therapist.

I sense *he* sensed I had struggled with all this for his sake, which was true; a sign of my concern he began to believe was genuine (and thus a little dangerous). I began, when appropriate, to playfully challenge some of his certainties regarding his 'odious' relational needs; he dropped the snarky quips, and began relating his dreams, with both humor and a candor I came to deeply appreciate.

***

Absurdity is king, but love saves us from it.

(Camus, 1963, p. 93)

Conclusion

One of the many absurdities found in this clinical illustration points to the ways in which archaically unilluminated experience enters the dyadic picture, as participants' self-protections become intertwined. It is as if the relationship itself must at one time or another 'survive' mutual, asymmetrical disappointments, in order to discover that the relational center holds, with the horizon-line of understanding clearer after the storm clouds pass.

I worked to help Russ, for instance, work towards what he dreaded: the relational home he wanted and distrusted, with yearnings accompanied always by the potential voids of abandonment and/or scalding shame. Such danger led to his pulling away, which in turn led to my own self-protective distancing, leaving Russ on his own, again. (There remains, again, an almost cruel sort of comfort within one's *known* abandonments.) The absurdity of a patients' experiencing these types of retraumatization, which they have longed to do away with, speaks volumes about the paradoxes of our Sisyphean profession. Such absurdities include the ways in which we unwittingly hurt or disappoint patients we hope to help, and the ways patients seek to accommodate us, sometimes long before we catch on.

I find it important to keep these dilemmas in mind, as relationality itself is so foreign to many patients (as my patients' subjectivities are to me, initially at least). Some are even made repetitively anxious by the frame itself, in keeping appointment times, paying fees, stopping on time, and so on. Consider the complex absurdities, for instance, found within both Tish's disappointment in my lack of 'answers,' and my fearing her abandonment of *me*—after she had come to me with the hope of liberating *herself* from enslaving relationships!

We ask much of our patients, in many ways; they also, for instance, help us earn a living, have a practice, a career, and so on. Is this partially why, I wonder, I sometimes go a few minutes past a session's stop time, as if wanting to compensate for my dependence on *them*—together with the fact that I can never *totally* 'heal' or eradicate their trauma, help them 'get over it and move on'? Perhaps an essential aspect of relational home-building involves acknowledging, sooner or later, how we analysts cannot be enough, that the opportunity for *exact* parental attunement and the power to regulate affect is gone and cannot be salvaged, and that 'no effort whatsoever can change this fact' (Miller, 1979, p. 74). In this sense we become for certain patients an 'anti-Godot' (Haber, 2018) who will not arrive today, nor tomorrow, or ever.

Similarly, analysts may find the work more challenging or deflating than expected, when stumbling across some previously unforeseen vulnerabilities. Miller (1979) believes the latter *has* to happen (as does Kohut (1971, 1984)), for analysts to have a clearer empathic horizon of understanding, a dyadic presence that 'gives room' for patients' authenticities to emerge.

Thus, the importance of continuing our own parallel processes, as patients, as we grieve our own traumatic losses—sometimes provoked, I have found, by the very asymmetry of the analytic relationship itself, which can recreate the 'little caregiver' scenario with eerie precision. Per Atwood (2015), experiencing such grief is paramount; 'nothing else will do' (p. 151).

Miller (1979) comments that such grief involves a Camusian 'rebellion and mourning' (p. 54) aroused by our own awakening to our archaic abandonment or abuse. This rebellion might include the self-expression of long-disavowed sorrow, anger, or rage, our own awkward individuation. All of this becomes part of what we endure for patients (Orange, personal communication, 2018), in maintaining an open space or 'canvas' for patients' authentic self-expression.

Camus helps me see that the overwhelming pain of the losses described here stems in part from the profound expansiveness of the longings themselves. It would not hurt so much but that our need for relational safety, and attachment, is so foundational. The losses represented by absurd finitude cut against the infinite reach of unmet yearnings—death itself possibly becoming a forever-repeating, non-negotiable 'repetition.' Such permanence might imply, as it did for me as a youngster, becoming unthinkably 'lost' or unseen, *eternally*—floating in the void of death like a lonely astronaut, cut off from the eternally inattentive or absent other. Again, I think of Camus in regard to his detached mother, within a worldhood of dissociated, fog-like relatedness.

Perhaps this contributes to Camus' infamous womanizing, an antidotally, repetitively compulsive attempt at an (antidotal) intimacy that self-destructs even as it begins. This compulsion appeared to 'soothe' the agony of absent parents, as well as the demands of loyalty to the cramped and impoverished family from Algiers. (There is much to be said about the absurdity of addiction or compulsivity, as Brandchaft (2010) also indicated.)

Such antidotal maneuvering did catch up with him, causing no end of strife (including the attempted suicide of his second wife (Todd, 1998)). After this early mid-life crisis, however, he found a new expansiveness, relational and creative—cruelly halted by the fatal absurdity of his car accident. He was discovered amidst the wreckage with a look of horror on his face (Lottman, 1997), as though registering the fatal shock of finitude.

Fortunately, we have at least fragments of his final novel, about remembrance and sorrow, reminding me again of Camus' perseverance, reminding us that simply carrying on from one day to the next can itself be remarkable, as the narrator of *The Fall* (1956/1984) points out.

Essential to such continuing is the passion and creativity he reflects upon so eloquently in *The Myth of Sisyphus,* quoting Nietzsche regarding the necessity of finding 'something for which it is worth the trouble of living … something that transfigures … delicate, mad, or divine' (1942/1983, p. 64). I believe analysis is just such a divine madness, at times even a lost cause. However, like Camus I have a fondness for lost causes.

Psychoanalysis, after all, provides a liberating opportunity to gruelingly reclaim a forbidden emotional life, as patients painfully begin to acknowledge the harrowing solitary confinement they have endured, within a context that failed to acknowledge such suffering. Such an often-agonizing process leads, we hope, to a dyadic 'home' within which relatedness and authenticity might awaken, a process both beautiful and tragic. The process points to a horizon of sorrowful joy, containing both everything and nothing, as 'absurdity and beauty are [children] of the same earth' (1942/1983, p. 122).

References

Atwood, G.E. (2015). Credo and reflections. *Psychoanalytic Dialogues*, 25: 137–152.

Atwood, G.E. & Stolorow, R.D. (1993). *Faces in a cloud: Intersubjectivity in personality theory.* Lanham, MD: Jason Aronson, Inc.

Blatty, W.P. (Producer) & Friedkin, W. (Director). (1973). *The Exorcist.* USA: Warner Brothers.

Brandchaft, B. (1991). Countertransference in the analytic process. *Progress in Self Psychology*, 7: 99–105.

Brandchaft, B. (1994). To free the spirit from its cell. In R.D. Stolorow, G.E. Atwood, & B. Brandchaft (Eds.), *The intersubjective perspective* (pp. 57–74). Northvale, NJ: Jason Aronson.

Brandchaft, B. (2010). Systems of pathological accommodation in psychoanalysis. In B. Brandchaft, S. Doctors, & D. Sorter, *Toward an emancipatory psychoanalysis: Brandchaft's intersubjective vision* (pp. 193–220). New York: Routledge.

Bromberg, P. (1998). Staying the same while changing: Reflections on clinical judgment. *Psychoanalytic Dialogues*, 8(2): 225–236.

Camus, A. (1942/1983). *The Myth of Sisyphus* (J. O'Brien, trans.). New York: Alfred A. Knopf.

Camus, A. (1942/1988). *The Stranger* (M. Ward, trans.). New York: Alfred A. Knopf.

Camus, A. (1956/1984). *The Fall* (J. O'Brien, trans.). New York: Alfred A. Knopf.

Camus, A. (1963/2010). *Journals: 1935–1942* (P. Thody, trans.). Chicago: Ivan Dee.

Doctors, S. (2017). Brandchaft's pathological accommodation: What it is and what it isn't. *Psychoanalysis, Self and Context*, 12(1): 45–59.

Ferenczi, S. (1932/1988). *The clinical diary of Sandor Ferenczi*, J. Dupont (Ed.). Cambridge: Harvard University Press.

Haber, D. (2018). Yearning for Godot: Repetition and vulnerability in psychoanalysis. *Psychoanalysis, Self and Context*, 13(2): 132–148.

Kaplan, A. (2016). *Looking for The Stranger: Albert Camus and the life of a literary classic* [Kindle edition]. University of Chicago Press. Available on www.amazon.com.

Kohut, H. (1971). *The restoration of the self.* University of Chicago Press.

Kohut, H. (1984). *How does analysis cure?* University of Chicago Press.

Lottman, H. (1997). *Albert Camus: A Biography.* Corte Madera, CA: Gingko Press.

Miller, A. (1979). The drama of the gifted child and the psychoanalyst's narcissistic disturbance. *International Journal of Psychoanalysis*, 60: 47–58.

Orange, D.M. (2008). Whose shame is it anyway?: Lifeworlds of humiliation and systems of restoration (Or 'The analyst's shame'). *Contemporary Psychoanalysis*, 44(1): 83–100.

Orange, D.M. (2010). *Thinking for clinicians: Philosophical resources for contemporary psychoanalysis and the humanistic psychotherapies.* New York: Routledge.

Orange, D.M. (2011). *The suffering stranger: Hermeneutics for everyday clinical practice.* New York: Routledge.

Stern, D.B. (2003). *Unformulated experience: From dissociation to imagination.* New York: Routledge.

Stolorow, B. & Stolorow, R.D. (2011, November 17). Blues, trauma, finitude [blog post]. Retrieved from www.huffingtonpost.com/robert-d-stolorow/blues-trauma-fini tude_b_553256.html.

Stolorow, R.D. (1999). Antidotes, enactments, rituals, and the dance of reassurance: Comments on the case of Joanna Churchill & Alan Kindler. *Progress in Self-Psychology*, 15: 229–232.

Stolorow, R.D. (2007). *Trauma and human existence.* New York: Analytic Press.

Stolorow, R.D. (2011). *World, affectivity, trauma: Heidegger and post-Cartesian psychoanalysis.* New York: Routledge.

Stolorow, R.D. (2015). A phenomenological-contextual, existential, and ethical perspective on emotional trauma. *Psychoanalytic Review*, 102: 123–138.

Stolorow, R.D. & Atwood, G.E. (1984). *Structures of subjectivity: Explorations in psychoanalytic phenomenology and contextualism.* New York: Routledge.

Stolorow, R.D. & Atwood, G.E. (1992). *Contexts of being: The intersubjective foundations of psychological life*. Hillsdale, NJ: The Analytic Press.

Stolorow, R.D. & Atwood, G.E. (2016). Walking the tightrope of emotional dwelling. *Psychoanalytic Dialogues*, 26: 103–108.

Stolorow, R.D. & Schwartz, J.M. (2002). Worlds of trauma. In R.D. Stolorow, G.E. Atwood, & D.M. Orange, *Worlds of experience: Interweaving philosophical and clinical dimensions in psychoanalysis* (pp. 123–138). New York: Basic Books.

Todd, O. (1998). *Albert Camus: A life* (B. Ivry, trans.) [Kindle version]. New York: Knopf. Available from www.amazon.com.

Winnicott, D.W. (1965). The maturational processes and the facilitating environment: studies in the theory of emotional development. *The International Psycho-Analytical Library*, 64: 1–276. London: The Hogarth Press and the Institute of Psycho-Analysis.

Zaretzky, R. (2013). *A life worth living: Albert Camus and the quest for meaning*. Harvard University Press.

Chapter 4

Lost in Reflection

Winnicottian Mirroring and Invisibility in Early Caregiving

Introduction

Though not traditionally categorized as 'relational,' the later work of D.W. Winnicott reveals an increasingly relational sensibility, as elaborated in *Playing and Reality* (1971). Such ideas, elegantly yet obliquely expressed, 'suggest possibilities of meaning' (Ogden, 2001, p. 300). They also resonate with my own chosen theory of intersubjective-systems, including Brandchaft's (2010) notion of pathological accommodation, a sibling to Winnicott's false-self compliance.

In this chapter I look at Winnicott's idea of the mirror-role of caregivers, including its application in a difficult case—specifically, how its absence leads to an invisibility of the infant's affectivity and a subsequent self-annihilating, inflexible compliance to the needs of others. An early environment's failure to deeply, affectively see or existentially recognize the child's presence, the wonder or awe of its arrival—in favor for instance of a more mechanical or performative approach—ever foregrounds the needs of others, traumatically blurring embodied presence.

As an example, I describe a treatment occurring within a constricting analytic space I somehow co-created with an acutely depressed patient. Here both of our subjectivities became, to paraphrase Winnicott, looked at rather than into, obscuring both of us. I came to see my own analytic invisibility and resulting transference as analogous to the patient's, a woman never existentially recognized by anyone—aside from, a bit belatedly, her analyst.

> When I look I am seen, so I exist.
>
> (Winnicott, 1971, p. 114)

The Empty Mirror

Winnicott states the mirror-role begins in the earliest of days, when the infant finds the mother's face, and sees 'himself or herself ... [as] the mother

DOI: 10.4324/9781003266358-5

is looking at the baby, and what [the mother] looks like is related to what she sees there' (Winnicott, 1971, p. 112, italics original). Does the baby in other words find some embodiment of love, awe, or something more akin to impatience or anxiety?

Winnicott notes the mother/caregiver also sees herself seen by the baby, thus setting a relational atmosphere of responsiveness (hopefully) and fundamental attunement.

Eigen (1981) suggests we not read Winnicott too literally, to use our clinical imaginations in making sense of his ideas. In my own reading, I envision a primitively tender mutuality between caregiver and infant, ever oscillating, the earliest stirrings of the relational dance. The 'background music' becomes the affective ambience or backdrop of the environment, be it soothing, fraught, or something else.

Here we find paradox, a shared worldhood influenced by a pairing of neither two nor one, as in the asymmetrical mutuality of analysis itself. Winnicott asks that caregivers and analysts respect this paradox, rather than overly influence or attempt to control the outcome.

I sometimes try to imagine the affective tonality and subsequent dynamic of patients' earliest worlds. Babies welcomed for both their beauty and distress (and messy bodily functions), find safety in the attuned oscillation between near-merger and nascent autonomy: a safely flexible reliance, nurturing the baby's budding development.

Patients' affective processes offer hints of their distinctive early environments, and caregivers' (in)tolerance of dependence and separation, as babies experience the earliest stirrings of personhood, without (one hopes) demands for caregivers' recognition. An early relational distancing or misattunement is implied for instance, when patients relate trauma-like reactions to their own children's differentiation, perhaps never experienced or handled lovingly in their earliest days. This applies to the case study I shall present, where the patient struggled to tolerate and nurture her daughter's differentiation, after a childhood wherein *her* mother was overwhelmed, even repulsed by her daughter's needs, starting (I surmised) in infancy. My patient Jean's early intimacy with her own children was the closest loving contact ever experienced by her, as her teenage daughter's differentiation became akin to abandonment, even as the patient knew she 'ought' not to feel this way and instead responsibly parent, which for her was akin to speaking in some unknown mother tongue.

***

Winnicott states that a reliably safe environment is essential for the infant's entire 'emotional and mental development' (1971, p. 112). Babies must have a good-enough primitive welcome, facilitating their 'existing, not reacting' (Winnicott, 1965, p. 145). (Some patients learn to live in reactivity.) Infant research confirms the Winnicottian notion that attuned responsiveness recognizes as real (Nahum, 1994) the baby's embodied perceptions and experiences, lending a 'vital coherence' (Sander, quoted in Nahum, 1994, p. 3) to germinal selfhood.

We might imagine this process as cyclical and expansive rather than linear, as Kohut (1984) describes a person's evolving needs for responsiveness, across a lifetime of fluid relatedness. My emphasis is on a *lived* affectivity—caregivers do not for instance observe some thing called 'goodness'—the baby itself *is* good, is love, within the goodness of a caring surround, embodied and lived in the pairing. Such intersubjectivity is what Winnicott was beginning to suggest later in his career, I believe.

Such recognition is ideally echoed throughout the life cycle. Yet, at the start, a rigid environment insisting on performative 'goodness' sets the stage for a deflated autonomy, leading to accommodation or compliance and even a possibly self-sabotaging rebellion, which I see often in working with addicted teens and young adults.

Winnicott recognizes caregiving as difficult and demanding of mothers/caregivers. Yet an early environmental anxiety, demanding reflection of *caregivers'* importance, can collapse the infant's (or patient's) potentiality (Ogden, 1985). It can also deflate the baby's omnipotence, another famously complex Winnicott-ism. We have here again a paradox that infants sense they control everything, including caregiver(s), in an environment facilitated by the latter. This delicate dance (Winnicott, 1971) is a necessary illusion of sorts, disastrous for development if punctured prematurely.

Dependence eases over time (ideally), along with the tender illusion of control, which infants incrementally surrender in tolerating gaps between their call and caregivers' response. Too long a delay—or anxious hovering—can lead to abandonment trauma, agentic crippling, or other developmental disruption. All of this emphasizes the hopefully-recognized basic goodness of the child's presence and existence, in a dynamically empathic attunement. (The notion of 'good enough' has been of great relief to me as a parent.)

Winnicott sees the mirror-role as analogous to therapy itself, a 'long-term giving the patient back what the patient brings,' so the patient will 'be able to exist *and to feel real*' (both Winnicott, 1971, p. 117, italics mine). The analyst like the caregiver serves as the 'constitutive witness' of true selfhood (Phillips, quoted in Nahum, 1984, p. 9); otherwise true selfhood is 'driven into hiding' (p. 9).

One can begin to imagine, then, an environment that does not recognize or reflect in such a way, exiling an infant into the 'primitive agonies' (Winnicott, 1974, p. 104) of painfully derailed strivings—which can lead, if not resolved, to stubbornly recurrent feeling-states of overwhelm or depressive futility, where 'nothing matters and life is not worth living' (Winnicott, 1971, p. 65).

I often observe this in my practice, with patients such as Jean, whose existence was contingent upon her vigilant responsiveness to others. Her own affectivity was consistently reflected as worthless, even toxic. I deeply suspected her early caregivers insisted on the recognition of *their* needs; Jean's mother, even now, stated to her daughter in phone conversations that babies were 'disgusting.' Jean often, via dissociative rumination, appeared hellbent on making herself small around others, or invisible, to avoid becoming a target, even with her analyst. And with her alcoholic father, who demanded the recognition of his worthiness, angrily negating anything less.

Jean thus yearned for being seen and recognized, at the same time warding off this most fundamental (and risky) need for responsive recognition, resulting in a 'split' selfhood, forever fracturing her perspective in favor of others, rigidly compelling her to provide for all but herself. This landed us in a logjam from the first session, since 'the patient comes first' in analysis: more foreign code for Jean, as I myself became (like all others in her life) a mirror to be looked *at* rather than into (Winnicott, 1971).

Message in a Bottle

When Jean, a slender, attractive, and anxiously depressed woman in her late forties, first arrived at my office, she despaired that her husband Will would abandon her, due to the agony her depression caused *him*. He stated her 'laziness' was the true cause of her depression, a conviction she echoed. Such shaming criticism and wounded protest (should anyone push back on him) represented her husband's entire relational repertoire; which in her case consisted mostly of accommodation or rebellious withdrawal.

Jean had given up her career to raise her children. She now focused upon her teenage son, Zach, with an older daughter in college. Will was exasperated at her depression, with mounting psychiatry and therapy bills, as housekeeping duties lagged.

'What's for dinner tonight?' he would ask, shortly after breakfast. He saw such tasks as demonstrative of respect, given the wealth he alone had generated (as he frequently reminded Jean). He also denied a sneakily growing dependence on Xanax, which Jean astutely noticed with bemused irony.

The more she told me about herself, the more astonishing to me that depression had not paralyzed her sooner; it was her resilience and not any so-called weakness that impressed me, her self-hatred to the contrary. She blamed herself meanwhile for her son's marijuana addiction, even as Zach sounded like his father in his demands and blaming of Jan. This added to her surety that she was 'ruining the family' by 'bringing everyone down.' (Inarguably true for the longest time.)

When treatment started, Zach was attending an out-of-state program for teen drug use. Jean dreaded being alone in the house with her volatile husband. Zach meanwhile would call her, fast becoming irate in waiting for Jean to 'snap out of it.' This seemed to confirm her own inarguable failure as a mother, as did her academically successful older daughter, Claire, with an obsessive-compulsive perfectionism and borderline anorexia, requiring therapy and medication, all of which was (per Will) too fucking expensive.

Jean struck me as rigidly concrete, her relatedness ever performative—as if her affective life had never been recognized or made real, in the ways Winnicott describes. When she was little, her parents' fights grew so violent that she hid under the bed until the storm ended, usually with her father running off to the saloon, her mother weeping in the kitchen. Thus, mother again ended up in the spotlight. Jean fell asleep under the bed sometimes, a makeshift fortress, clinging to her stuffed animals. Or she might brew tea and comfort her mother, with words learned from television.

When Jean was 12, her father abruptly departed for good.

'She's all yours, I can't stand her,' he announced, throwing two suitcases into the back of his pickup truck, peeling away.

Jean watched from the front porch, bereft, not knowing if or when she would see him again. (She would, intermittently.) What she remembered most was her mother's wailing inside the house.

This tragedy was eclipsed years later, during her first pregnancy, when her inebriated father crashed into a ditch, the car aflame. Jean was called at midnight to identify the charred corpse, a most harrowing image. Yet, while admittedly devastated, she again expressed sadness for *him*, since 'Dad missed out, he always wanted grandkids.' (She blamed mechanical failure for the accident.)

I asked if such unspeakable loss might relate to her current depression, including abandonment possibly provoked by her son's departure for rehab. A parallel depression had also occurred when her daughter left for college.

'Maybe, so how do I fix it?' she asked.

Jean had no interest in affective exploration; she was desperate for relief *now*. The past was past, her family needed her, and 'why isn't the medication working?'

Still, I gave it the old college try, wondering if I was hearing the little girl under the bed, who yearned to be seen, heard.

Jean nearly shouted, 'She needs to pipe down and grow up!' I was stunned, noting privately that her depression was in a way her most authentic dimension, echoing dolefully across the chasm of a long-abandoned selfhood.

Meanwhile my empathic explorations went (mostly) nowhere, with Jean oscillating between self-loathing, a fleeting wish to be treated better at home, and the terror that she would never improve.

Then, one bright morning, after a long weekend, she stated that she was feeling better. She smiled and said, 'I am so, so grateful … for my psychiatrist.' The right medication had been found. The transformation was stunning.

This pharmaceutical miracle brightened the room; she said, quite pleased, that the 'whiny' little girl had finally shut up. I had to dissuade her from cutting back or ending treatment altogether, astonished at how ready she was to terminate.

From there, things proceeded pleasantly enough, though she seemed disinterested on exploring or understanding a depression now thankfully gone.

She revealed a charming and engaging side, previously unseen, relating amusing anecdotes from the news, with occasional references to her husband's savage criticisms, usually dismissed with the comment, 'he is who he is, you can't change anybody.' A consideration not given to herself, alas.

I was torn here, as she enjoyed my company, and vice-versa, even as her mostly giddy mood contrasted almost eerily with her earlier anguish, as if that 'version' of Jean—the little girl—remained locked away. I shared some gentle curiosity about this, which drew a blank stare.

Then the roof fell in again. Zach, returned from rehab, was caught smoking and sharing pot with friends at school, which gave him one last chance at probation if he again sought treatment, and drug-tested clean for the remainder of the school year. Otherwise, expulsion.

Will, an alumnus of this prestigious private school, was apoplectic, again laying blame on Jean's head, as Zach raged about the unfairness of his school's reaction and how Jean's depression 'fucked me up,' with Will hammering her about the cost of rehab. Her worried daughter volunteered to leave school to look after Jean, which Will adamantly opposed.

'Please,' Jean said to me, 'I cannot be depressed again!'

She repeated this like a mantra, wondering what she had to do to improve, besides my useless suggestion of resting and going easy on herself. I occasionally, wearily, offered other suggestions, even as I saw again the neglected girl under the bed, hiding from her raging family, as vulnerability remained hidden. (In a way I felt under there with her.) She then told me, out of a frustrated fear, that she might terminate analysis, in favor of trans-magnetic stimulation.

Then she began missing sessions randomly. This surprised then irritated me, as she ran errands for everyone under the sun, even her neighbor, in attempting to demonstrate her worth. I wanted to defend the importance of our work, without sounding too demanding: an impossible high-wire act. I made solemn statements to her about the importance of analysis, the only place in her life where she was free to be herself. Yet I knew it was thin even as I uttered the words, as 'being herself' was inarguably toxic, anathema to her survival.

Finally, after yet another absence, I spontaneously shared with her my exasperation. I wondered at the start of the session why she was treating me like chopped liver. She found this amusing.

'Aw c'mon,' she said, 'you're a professional! Don't take it personally.'

Noting my confusion, she explained that, yes she sometimes blew off sessions, and sorry but she had to. I playfully challenged this. She countered that, after all, I still got paid. Like Will pays you, I thought, astonished again at the transactional nature of her existence, the mechanization of all affectivity.

I noted the pressure she was under, but that I could not help her mitigate such intensity, likely adding to the depression, if she did not show up. I then added, with a tenderness that surprised me, that I cared less about the money and more about her treatment.

'And,' I said, with a gentle firmness, 'about you.' I pointed at her for emphasis.

Her eyes widened as if startled, before her demeanor softened; how rarely had she received such recognition!

She seemed to take this in, gently shaken; soon after, her disappearances stopped almost entirely.

Sought and Found

Jean told me over subsequent sessions that her depression had again started to lift. I better understood the pressure upon her to survive, via 'an impersonal imperative for action,' versus a menaced authenticity which 'must be got rid of.' (both Ogden, 1985, p. 134). Such had been her way of life from the beginning.

But not only hers. For I, too, noticed how the dark gravity of her tumult had provoked some of my own archaic self-organization and unseen experience. In my upbringing, I became a 'little analyst' (Atwood, 2015) to two compromised caregivers, including an alcoholic father. The spontaneously playful, expressive child I hoped to be was dangerous, even forbidden. With Jean, I felt prohibited from being the *analyst* I hoped to be, in accommodating her accommodations, which began to chafe, even irritate. Will furthermore reminded me of my father, provoking a somewhat reactive desire to protect her, via my suggestions of ways she could defend herself—which she reactively organized as more 'tasks.' Thus we recreated her home dynamic to a degree, even as I struggled not to do so. She was aware of her inability to better protect herself—but not the paralyzing, repeated trauma at the center, thus reinforcing her sense of inadequacy and reactive provision. I found a way to address this via a playful forcefulness, in underlining her importance to me, and of my needing her reliable presence to help her heal. She had in other words to show up for herself, *with* rather than strictly *for* someone.

Jean's self-censoring loosened incrementally, as transferential fog began to clear, at least in this early stage of the alliance.

She one day astonished me by noting, 'I'm always treated like a fuckin' slave.'

We explored ways she might say 'no' to others, at least occasionally, me observing the danger for her of setting limits.

'I want Will to stop blaming me for everything,' she said, 'I'm trying the best I can.'

She managed to ask him to stop screaming when he became shrill, amazed at how quickly he backed off (while storing resentment that would eventually erupt). The decision to do this was hers; she had to come to it on her own.

This is the faith (Eigen, 1981) that Winnicott asks us to put in patients, or dyadic process, until the patient finds it safe or necessary enough to manifest re-integration, engage more expansively, self-protect against abusiveness and so on: a gradual expansion of permeability that gathers its own momentum in the empathically reflective environment of analysis.

Conclusion

Winnicott observed that 'the analyst's function is survival' (1971, p. 136). In this case, I scrambled to survive a chaotic intersubjective constriction, which seemed initially to reflect my own insignificance, an echo of archaic invisibility. I felt invisible with Jean, swallowed up by her chaos, which paralyzed me. In fact, the rapport we developed while discussing apparently trivial things turned out to be vital later, when I employed humor to confront her absences. Such disappearances seemed to disappear me, leading to a somewhat dramatic need to defend my analytic presence and our process. One could say I had to differentiate from the patient's context, to breathe life back into our potential space.

Perhaps Jean had to enact her disappearance as a way of communicating her cosmic insignificance. See? I can't show up for myself. I'm not really here … or anywhere. She disappeared behind her compliant smile like the Cheshire Cat. My belated emphasis on her importance to me, as a person and not only a patient, as I more deeply sensed her enslavement, was genuine and unexpected, and seemed to underline for her a recognition, and sense of worthiness—even after she had 'messed up' and disappointed someone (her analyst) yet again.

Behind her compulsive caregiving, her archaically-instilled enslavement, Jean had always yearned for someone to reflect her existential beneficence, with a terror of permanent exile—a striving both sought and averted. But such forestalled affectivity 'came due' eventually, erupting into a raging depression when her children left home, especially her beloved younger child, who left her alone with her husband, as had happened when her father abandoned her to her mercurial mother.

In my disconfirming the rage she usually encountered, after her absences began to frustrate me (which she must, in some way, have noticed), and I 'called her out' without condemning her, she began to trust at least the seedlings of a relational home (Stolorow, 2007), where she was reflected as worthy, as *good*, without being discarded or viciously condemned.

Winnicott emphasizes that patients manifest their authenticity (or true self, in his words) in their own way and time. The emotional turbulence caused by feelings of our invisibility to patients, a sense of our being unseen or 'used' as they themselves have been, can subvert our own quiet need to be seen—as effective, analytically benevolent, or having faith in the patient's potential. Such a need is easily overlooked by us when 'it's about the patient and only the patient' becomes rigid orthodoxy. Sometimes in supervision, I find helpful such statements as, 'boy you really care about this patient' or 'this is tough because she can't let you see her.'

Relational home building can be grueling, as Winnicott (1971) also notes. The empathic giving back of the patient's struggle to exist, to be there safely, is often fiercely resisted even as it is sought, as we ask patients in a sense to shed the armor that has saved them from fatal wounding. There is temptation to reach for our own conceptual armor, when we sense pushback or the squeeze of transferential demands.

Analysis, however transformative, cannot fully 'erase' or heal archaic wounding. Analysis makes space for such agony, a mourning of what was lost, though we cannot literally recreate archaic circumstances.

I discovered this in parenting, in the love and trust of my child, both radiant and reflective of a grimly contrasted archaic abandonment and neglect, never acknowledged by caregivers, still surprisingly raw, even amidst current moments of joy. Such rawness was not healed, only recognized, and mourned as a long-unseen injury. This better prepared me however in understanding patients such as Jean, in her terror of her children's differentiation, which she knew she 'ought' to encourage, even as it distressed her. Such dissonance is characteristic of early surrounds where the child comes to question or doubt their own unseen or condemned affectivity, whether it is 'real.' In this way we bring patients to life through and not around unspeakable pain, challenging familiarity.

Gradually, through and via our analytic tumult, Jean and I found each other. She recognized my recognition, increasing trust while enabling more playfulness, humor, and affective flexibility. Our relationship managed to, in Winnicottian terms, survive the intersubjective attack of mutually-provoked self-protections. She persisted through difficult work, over many years. Perhaps any analysis worth its salt also, over time and in unexpected ways, gives back to the analyst what the latter desires: some measure of asymmetrical recognition, usually preceded by the patient's defensive devaluing or deflation. Yet even this can help us, in understanding the latter as analogous to the patient's trauma, what has necessitated fierce self-protectiveness, so often observed or felt before fully seen—like the forgotten child hiding in plain sight all along.

References

Atwood, G.E. (2015). Credo and reflections. *Psychoanalytic Dialogues*, 25(2): 137–152.

Brandchaft, B. (2010). Systems of pathological accommodation in psychoanalysis. In S. Doctors & D. Sorter (Eds.), *Toward an emancipatory psychoanalysis: Brandchaft's intersubjective vision* (pp. 193–220). New York: Routledge.

Eigen, M. (1981). The area of faith in Winnicott, Lacan and Bion. *International Journal of Psychoanalysis*, 62: 413–433.

Kohut, H. (1984). *How does analysis cure?* Chicago: University of Chicago Press.

Nahum, J. (1994). New theoretical vistas in psychoanalysis: Louis Sander's theory of early development. *Psychoanalytic Psychology*, 11(1): 1–19.

Ogden, T.H. (1985). On potential space. *International Journal of Psychoanalysis*, 66: 129–141.

Ogden, T.H. (2001). Reading Winnicott. *Psychoanalytic Quarterly*, 70(2): 299–323.

Stolorow, R.D. (2007). *Trauma and human experience*. Oxon, UK: Routledge.

Winnicott, D.W. (1965). *The maturational processes and the facilitating environment: Studies in the theory of emotional development*. Madison, CT: International Universities Press.

Winnicott, D.W. (1971). *Playing and reality*. Oxon, UK: Routledge.

Winnicott, D.W. (1974). Fear of breakdown. *International Review of Psycho-Analysis*, 1(1-2): 103–107.

Chapter 5

Accommodating Brandchaft

Theory and Transference in Analytic Training

Introduction

How are we to work with pathological (or unconscious) accommodation, as Brandchaft (2010) calls it, especially when such emotional processes operate at pre-reflective, often deeply protected, levels of a person's subjectivity? Brandchaft, ever-prescient, understood these processes to be formed because they were essential for a person's psychological survival, in order to 'sustain a belief in the continuity of his or her own existence' (2010, p. 200). Often, such processes remain stubbornly unconscious, with a 'do or die' mission to defend rigid perceptual and emotional convictions that ensure ongoing ties to attachment figures—both in the archaic surround and, later, in psycho-analysis. Working with such patients can be a halting and challenging process. As Brandchaft noted, '[t]he extent to which any particular analyst, at any particular moment, is free from imprisoning attachments of his own ... remains the decisive, and by no means settled, issue' (2010, p. 198).

Accommodative patients often become terrified at the merest stirrings of their own expansiveness, which of course are *non*-accommodative and may lead to 'fundamental differentiating change' (2010, p. 199), challenging archaic beliefs and rocking the relational boat. Any spark of desire or vita-lizing affect that reflects spontaneous selfhood is perceived as a potential iceberg that might sink said boat, and must be averted to prevent catastrophe.

The picture is further complicated when similar processes characterize the *analyst's* subjectivity and its possibly unreflected expression in the analysis. In the end, tracking, illuminating and working through these intersubjective 'intertwinings' in the transference—both analysand's and analyst's—is the challenge of the work.

Bernard Brandchaft, in his seminal writing (2010) on the subject, incisively describes the intersubjective rootedness of unconscious accommodation devel-oping within a surround that demands the infant/child's pitch-perfect attune-ment to caregivers' 'insecure attachment patterns' (p. 206) and utter allegiance to the system's 'abstract depersonalized organizing principles' (p. 198). The

DOI: 10.4324/9781003266358-6

child adapts a hyper-sensitive attunement *to caregivers*, in order to satisfy the surround's endless demands. In such systems, the child risks abandonment or attack if he or she dares non-compliance. This leads to 'the exclusion of whole domains of the subjective reality of the child' (p. 199), thereby flattening the latter's distinctive affective experience and vitalizing sense of personhood. These commands and subsequent compliance become central to the child's (and later the analysand's) personality organization, including his or her developmental and repetitive organizing activity in analysis (Stolorow, Brandchaft & Atwood, 1987).

As Brandchaft well knew, some of the children forced to 'precociously' attune to caregivers grow up to be analysts themselves—many of whom hope to facilitate a healing process which *they* too have undergone, namely emancipation from constricting or killer organizing principles (Stolorow, 1999). Some of us 'Brandchaft babies' (Maduro, personal communication, 2014) appear to be a natural fit with acutely accommodative patients, since we have walked in their shoes after all. It also brings resonance in hearing patients feeling painfully unwelcome or unseen, due to matters of neurodivergence, race, gender, and so on, who are forced to accommodate an uncaring, unrecognizing social or professional surround.

This apparent fittedness is an aspect of conjunction between analyst and patient (Stolorow & Atwood, 1992), which can prove to be of immense therapeutic benefit to the dyad—provided the analyst continues to bring his *own* accommodative inclinations into reliable self-reflection. At the same time, we cannot catch everything; such an apparently organic fittedness can stoke the developmental hopes of an analyst eager to enlighten a fellow accommodator, as was the case with this newish analyst and his eager patient. It can be exciting to identify 'one of your own,' with the wish to stretch one's analytic wings.

Except that once again there is more here than meets the eye; such conjunctions may actually conceal therapeutic *dis*junctions, if for example an analyst's wish to liberate his accommodative patient—with Brandchaft 'coaching' the analyst from the wings—morphs into an archaically-rooted 'requirement' for the analyst's perfection. Analysts unfamiliar with the intensity of some patients' defensive processes (such as contempt) may find it hard to keep their footing, which can then provoke an analyst's defensive processing, fending off shame or self-doubt. Or a patient's longstanding allegiance to 'immutable beliefs' (Brandchaft, 2010, p. 203) might collide with the analyst's intentions, when for example a patient's rigidity disturbs the analyst, and paralyzes dyadic process. Predictably, the accommodatively-organized patient might experience the analyst's anxiety or hesitation as indices of *his or her own* 'failure,' cruelty or overall badness.

In short, a project of therapeutic emancipation can transform into dyadic gridlock, as analysand's and analyst's co-occurring transferences commingle in a way that threatens each participant, sending hopes of emancipation down the rabbit hole if unresolved.

This disjunction is further complexified when analysts hope to succeed with such patients, by successfully employing an analytic theory with which he is newly enamored—a developmental transference *with the theory itself.* This is a theme of the present chapter, which explores ways in which accommodatively-organized analysts are vulnerable to interpret prereflectively their chosen theory, as I did Brandchaft's in the case study discussed, as another set of commands, including the adoption of the theorist's apparently ever-patient, sagacious mien.

The brighter the illumination, the darker the shadow that trails behind: an initial desire to seek out a kinder, gentler 'caretaker' (which I found in the figure of Brandchaft), to foster the kind of expansive experience denied archaically, becomes transmogrified into yet another demand for the analyst to serve an authority figure. This repetitive experience of disappointing a distinguished mentor figure becomes poignantly ironic when the authority figure is Brandchaft and his theory of unconscious accommodation! In this disheartening disjunction, Brandchaft is perceived to command unrelenting compliance to his theory, lest his disciple make a muddle of it and cartwheel like Icarus into the sea.

Intriguingly however, this theory-transference paralleled the patient's experience of my 'disappointment,' organized as *his* failure to sufficiently serve *my* demands (much as he perceived himself as failing his wife), prompting his emotional withdrawal, which in turn heightened my anxiety and self-doubt, and so on: a thorny, self-reinforcing disjunction that threatened to send the treatment itself spiraling into the depths.

What would Bernie do?

Just before discovering Brandchaft at the start of my analytic candidacy, I was planning my exit from an upscale treatment center for addiction, where I worked as a residential counselor. An initially snug fit there had tightened like a noose.

The bedrock of the rehab was the 12-step philosophy as laid out in Alcoholics Anonymous, especially the 'Big Book' (2001), which we handed out to patients upon admittance. There was also a loose amalgam of CBT, DBT and other acronymic band-aids, but for the most part we tried to persuade patients to 'trust God and clean house' (Alcoholics Anonymous, 2001, p. 98).

My disillusion was an unpleasant surprise. At first, because I had personally benefited from recovery programs, the rehab provided a cozy conjunction with my personal and professional desires. However, there is a vast difference between entering recovery voluntarily (like myself and most staff) and being Shanghai'd into treatment by an interventionist, like most of our young-adult clientele, for whom immortality is necessarily illusory. I found the one-size-fits-all approach of AA used by staff as a kind of truncheon against 'rebellious' patients who wouldn't get in line—*accommodate*—our agenda. This rigidity and (subtle or overt) disapproval functioned as a *cordon sanitaire* (Stolorow, 2007) for *staff's* protection. Our agenda of compliance often meshed with the families who paid us, in a way that felt like collusion. Bradley Jones (2009) describes the pull for accommodation within AA, which matched my own disquieting observations in recovery settings.

At my job, patients showing signs of resistance were often labelled as narcissistic or borderline. These facile derogations marked, I believed, a clinical failure to understand our patients, as well as the limitations of a thirty-day treatment program. To apply the term 'addict' to all patients without much or (in some cases) any sustained empathic inquiry (Stolorow, Brandchaft & Atwood, 1987) was an error on our part, well-intentioned as my colleagues were. Social anxiety overlaid with shame, resulting from unrecognized trauma, is for instance not the same as 'defiance.'

I voiced these concerns in staff meetings, usually resulting in skepticism from supervisors who re-asserted our patients were suited only for counseling, not therapy. (I was never sure what this meant.) Such comments reminded me of some of my father's criticisms in childhood, including admonitions for me to enforce order with my younger siblings, who resented my attempts to control. (I was eight years old.) I felt caught in the middle, then and now—'overburdened,' Brandchaft called it (2010, p. 206), by non-negotiable demands.

It is hard to overstate how emancipating Brandchaft's writings were: here was a way to more accurately conceive so-called 'people-pleasing,' a recovery term I loathed, as it reflected an isolated-mind perspective (Stolorow & Atwood, 1992). In Brandchaft's work the idea was systematized in an *intersubjective* context that broadened perspective; one might, for instance, see admixtures of these tendencies and addiction occurring together. I had long felt that to see patients' issues occurring only *outside* their formative surrounds was myopic.

Brandchaft framed the problem in dynamic, *process*-based language that incisively articulated such early surrounds. The rehab's isolated-mind perspective seemed a key contributor to flinty enactments with patients; we deemed this in most cases to be 'acting out.'

Brandchaft's paper then led me to intersubjective-systems theory, which confirmed that the therapist's (or analyst's) perspective informs the process *much more* than we are aware, even those of us who admit to counter-transference.

Brandchaft showed how caregivers can subtly or overtly *demand* compliance from their children, instilling 'immutable belief systems' (2010, p. 197) or 'dictates of antiquity' (Browne, quoted in Brandchaft, 2010, p. 196) that remain formidable in treatment, leading possibly to enactment in the rehab setting. Such dictates and beliefs create an organizing imperative within the child's subjectivity to accommodate or risk losing relational ties. I'd long intuited, without having the words, that accommodation for some was a matter of life or death—not a weakness of character, but a means to 'sustain a belief ... *in his or her own existence*' (p. 200, italics mine). I'd stumbled upon a pile of (conceptual) gold, since finally *someone got it!*

Not only was I impressed by Brandchaft's authorial eloquence, which I hoped to emulate, but here also was a window into my own history. I had grown up in a family with many elephants in the room. Number one was my parents' failure to provide anything close to an attuned surround, as I was expected to attune to *them,* in taking care of my siblings and providing companionship to an alcoholic father, who required positive mirroring lest he lash out. Brandchaft called it, and I heard it for the first time, *relational trauma.*

'Trauma'—not 'exaggeration' or 'dramatics,' as I had long been told.

Except that is not the point of this chapter (so saith my 'critical voice,' sounding suspiciously paternal). *You turned out pretty well, and to attack your father, may he rest in peace, is a little cheap. Plus, this is supposed to be an* academic *endeavor, not an Oprah-ish 'memoir'!*

Do these criticisms originate from my father's castigations, whenever I dared complain? *There you go again! Remember that Mitchell (1988) and other theorists have pointed out that life is neither fair nor perfect. And harping on the past is spiritually unsound, remember your recovery! Resentment is fatal. Anyway is this a book chapter or the grinding of a few personal axes? You don't hear Brandchaft whining about 'daddy'!*

This is what I was up against.

A Perfect Fit

Initially we seemed a perfect fit, and our first few sessions appeared to bring relief from the anxiety attacks that brought him into treatment. Alan, 35, was referred to me by a psychiatrist who congratulated me on my private practice, promising more referrals 'if this one goes well.'

I was excited to have my first analysand, and soon observed patterns of unconscious accommodation—exactly what Brandchaft wrote about! Alan initially appeared responsive to my empathically reflecting his anxiety and the fear that it was permanent. He agreed to come three times a week: another confidence builder. But then I detected that the frequency fed an expectation that his troubles would be cleared up sooner rather than later, as I came to see us as mired in quicksand.

The climate in the room quickly darkened with smothering apprehension and dread. I soon sensed Alan disliked being there and *himself* for having to be there, as if the very need for treatment was a 'failure,' leading to a fiercely ambivalent attitude about same. He wondered if treatment would take long, while acknowledging his anxiety had diminished, a little—contingent on the hope of a rapid cure.

The *real* challenge, he informed me, was deciding whether or not to end an online dalliance started in a chatroom. Of course he should, yet couldn't. He and his internet 'mistress,' Wendy, whom he vaguely knew and started chatting with online, instant-messaged each other with increasing flirtation; he'd tried to stop but couldn't. He needed to be loyal to his wife, and here he was mutually masturbating with a married woman via Skype. It was pathetic, disgusting, and he couldn't wait to do it again.

He was also ashamed for wanting praise from Wendy, who told him he was 'strong,' 'manly.' When I reflected back to him the positive impact of these remarks, rarely heard at home, he snapped, 'I shouldn't need them.' *Hoh boy.* I detected an anxiously maintained self-ideal (Stolorow, 2007), needed to forego all personal satisfactions and pleasures in the name of loyalty, an immutable dictate of old. He held a metaphorical gun to his head; there was something disturbingly brutal about his subjective self-criticism.

His spouse, Karen, he told me, was 'probably an alcoholic'—but 'high functioning,' drinking only after work. He feared she'd discover his betrayal. She also had a savage tongue and temper, stoking his fear of aloneness and failure to provide the self-sacrifice life demanded. He was in quite the quandary in that he seemed to crave the intimacy (however 'virtual') that now represented betrayal to Karen, as if he needed to be *bulletproof* in deflecting all desires. He mostly feared this discovery would destroy her.

Furthermore, nearly any hurt feelings resulting from her criticisms was 'weakness' since it jeopardized his ability to accommodate—almost as if he wanted to be the Superman of self-sacrificing compliance. Anything short of this was inexcusable. He subtly then overtly began to demand of this of our work, that we find the teflon ASAP.

He both resented and agreed with the complaints Karen repeated, regarding money and sex. Money, because if he really 'cared about the marriage' he would find more work (as a freelance copywriter); sex, which he avoided since he found her unattractive while drunk. 'You sure it still works?' his wife would crack. Inwardly wincing, I asked if that was hurtful.

'She's under a lot of pressure at work,' he said flatly. 'Her boss is an asshole.'

And she isn't, with that remark? I nodded. 'So you ... "shouldn't" be upset?'

Ignoring this, he said Karen wanted to have children. He had mixed feelings. Because of her imbibing? I asked.

'Because I'd be a lousy father if I'm screwing around.'

'Sounds like the problems here are all your fault.'

He shrugged. 'We can only be responsible for ourselves.' Another indisputable truth.

At one point he uncomfortably described his enjoyment of Wendy's praises. I speculated it was nice to hear in light of his wife's criticisms. He shook his head in disagreement, then sighed somewhat dramatically. 'Is therapy always this depressing?'

'You're doing great,' I said impulsively. Something had gone off track. He then peppered me with questions about how 'all this talking' would help him get off the internet. So pointedly fraught was his inquiry that I began to feel my own empathic stance at issue, as if my curiosity were dangerous. Anxiety crept in and I became a bit frustrated. But then I recalled the balanced, wisely empathic tone of Brandchaft's writings, which I hoped to model, rather than 'blame the patient' for my own uncertainties.

At the same time, I suspected that what drove his questions was the hope of a 'riddance fantasy' (Stolorow, personal communication, 2013) that might purge all need and vulnerability, return him to normal, in this case his self-idealized (accommodative) state—as if he wanted to disconnect from his own authentically existential discomfort. Of course, he would be unhappy at home, with an often-drunk spouse who verbally rousted him. This then created distance, leading to his increased relational desire, which led to guilt over said distance and his total culpability.

Rather than join me in the *exploration* of such a vicious circle, and its possible connection to earlier developmental derailment, he sought 'aha!' insights which would speed things along, get rid of his desire for Wendy's attention, which was 'stupid' and caused trouble. Anything besides that implied a failure on, I now sensed, both our parts.

'Give yourself a break,' I said at one point, 'alcoholism is difficult to live with.'

'She's not an alcoholic,' he said hurriedly. Before I could respond, the questions renewed: 'Can you be addicted to a person, like with alcohol? How do the 12 steps "work"? Why do you have to make amends? Do I owe *her* an amends? Would it help if I made amends to her *right now*?'

Again the atmosphere thickened; I was unsure how to navigate. But I *should* know. I was, as he often reminded me, the 'professional.' We'd been meeting for almost two months after all. Yet we spoke different languages— he wanted results, *yesterday*. I began to vaguely resent the stonewalling that came along with his impatience and growing demands for 'answers.'

Yet he was new to individual therapy, let alone analysis, and that needed to be recognized. I tried to mirror his emotional courage, in the hope of nurturing an idealizing transference that briefly surfaced from time to time.

It went nowhere, as (in his view) he shouldn't have been in analysis in the first place, due to his online 'philandering.'

Once he asked me if hypnotherapy might 'get him' to have sex with his wife; he had tried the night before and could not get an erection, prompting Karen's slurry yet hurtful sarcasm.

I said, 'I take it you hope that if you have sex with her, she'll stop criticizing.'

He leaned back, arms crossed. 'We talked about all this last week.'

We did? 'Maybe you're just not turned on,' I said, 'given the constant criticism?'

'When did *that* stop a guy from fucking?'

I said, 'Maybe it's hard to be attracted to a wife who kicks you verbally in the balls.'

He thought a moment. 'My dad used to say I needed to "toughen up".'

Mine too. Not a pleasant recollection. 'How was it to hear that?' I said.

'We talked about this before,' he said, impatient again. 'I mean, look, life's tough.'

So is analysis. I said, 'Your wife is putting you in quite a pickle, Alan.'

'That's marriage for you.'

This puzzled me.

He smirked and said, 'Don't be naïve.' He then said, irritated, 'Maybe you forget how brutal it is out there, I mean it's Darwinian, kill or be killed. You're talking to people here in this nice office all day. You want me to soften up, share my "feelings"?'—he was practically sneering—'I do that and the people around me, *they'll fucking eat me alive!*'

I sat there, quietly stunned. *So much for idealization.* He then looked embarrassed, closing his eyes, lapsing into a kind of hypnoidal state.

'This is difficult,' he said to himself, repetitively, with an expression of dread and confusion, 'Why is this so difficult ... it shouldn't be ... why is this so goddamn difficult?'

Why indeed.

Dancing in the Dark

I felt stymied, both by how he wanted me to build him a table while he hid the tools and lumber, and my own inability to circumnavigate these roadblocks. What was my contribution? I returned to Brandchaft (2010), noting his suggestion to attune to 'the patient's affective shifts via a disciplined and sustained use of the empathic-introspective approach' (p. 229)—shifts I had seen numerous times in sessions with Alan: a flicker of tender affect or yearning that disappeared like a snuffed candle. These shifts were so jarring that I often lost my balance. What was *this* about? Rigidity between affect states, in part, which did not seem to communicate with one another. Meanwhile his self-ideal organized pain as weakness, such weakness reflecting a literal truth about the Darwinian state of the world, rather than his own trauma. I was perhaps leading him back into an affective lion's den, which he saw as concretely true. No wonder we were both on edge.

I privately observed how his empathy was always saved for others, such as Wendy—who he shamefully 'leaned on'—and Karen, whom he failed, even as no one really 'wins' with alcoholism. I was annoyed at both Wendy *and* Karen, especially the latter, for blaming everything on Alan; I found it increasingly difficult to hear of her verbal stonings. Of course, she herself had endured an abusive alcoholic father who may have molested her—though this added to his demands for loyalty, to protect her from all harm, and the shame over failing such monolithic expectations. Again, the lonely circularity of a closed system.

Yet Alan gradually was able to tolerate the tendrils of my empathic interest in his so-called 'weaknesses,' quiet stirrings wherein we dwelled within uncomfortable feeling-states ... before he became anxious or again irritated, as our session was going to 'ruin his day,' since he felt bad now, not good. I was tempted to wisecrack, 'Would it help if I wore a bikini?' so eroticized were his emotional cravings for intimacy, for the validation of his strength and, I suspected, his basic *goodness* through the eyes of an ever-present other. All of this he found in pornography, a fast-acting yet ephemeral self-restoration (Stolorow, Atwood & Orange, 2002)—a relief soon dissipated by shame and self-loathing, which then provoked another need for (eroticized) soothing, and so on and so forth and *how long does this take?*

Problematically for us, he still hoped our process would function with the same antidotal efficiency in, as he said, 'helping me find answers to which feel good,' even as it the experience of feeling 'bad' that might help us understand what to change.

At times I sensed an 'or else' lurking behind such hard-edged hope for rapidity (not uncommon in working with addiction or compulsivity)—as in, 'Give me the answer ... or I'll fall apart because *you didn't come through.*' I often did not know how to respond without offending him. Answers such as, 'I don't have a magic wand' or 'this is so hard for you, isn't it' felt condescending. Alan for all the difficulties described here, could be quite charming, often tenderly compassionate towards others, even myself, telling me he would miss me when I took vacations. I imagined his early context as volatile, as I observed sudden glimmers of terror in his eyes, or desperation, when we began to talk of his deprivation and *angst*. This then prompted however a kind of authoritative demand—from myself or him, or both (it was hard to tell)—that analysis serves as a kind of drive-thru rather than 'dragging on forever.'

Given my own recovery background, suggestions involving Al-anon or other outside support, to buttress his analysis, went nowhere. He solicited practical help while refusing it, which led to further self-flagellation. ('Now I'm fucking up in therapy, too.') There were fleeting moments where I missed the rehab, monotonously reading the rules to new patients from our welcome booklet.

Alan was also skittish about relating his history, insisting that 'psychology isn't always about the past, my problems are all in the present.' (So there.) I detected more shame here, as if he were wary of casting his parents (like Karen) in a bad light—more disloyalty! After reassuring him we were not going to play a blame game, he related some of his upbringing.

His father was an engineer, a consultant for the U.S. Army, a moody and critical man who was stingy with mirroring or warmth, preferring to swill beer while his criticism flew. His mother withdrew to her bedroom, sleeping or watching TV and taking Valium. She suffered migraines and was often out of commission, occasionally clinging to Alan or his little brother before withdrawing again. Both parents reacted anxiously or angrily if Alan dared ask for more than the emotional gruel doled out to him, if he received anything at all.

He once asked me, 'Does my telling you this mean I can give up porn faster?'

These recollections appeared painful, as he recalled abandonments that repeated in his current life. But then the anxious side-stepping: an insistence that his parents were 'good people,' *he* was the selfish one. His father after all was only instilling the toughness needed for a rough-and-tumble world, a world that preyed on those with addiction—to cybersex, for instance, which was why he had to 'figure out' how to stop. I noted empathically how he had to detach from his own emotionality to avoid perturbing his environment. He said in effect that other kids were homeless and starving abroad.

I switched tactics, mentioning it might help if we could understand *why* cybersexing was such a draw—might we unpack the yearnings driving the behavior?

He said, 'Isn't that obvious?'

I countered that sexuality contained a wealth of unconscious wishes and hopes that were very important to understand.

'You people like to make it complicated,' he said, sighing.

I nearly suggested we end early. I also sensed his keen anxiety, that his fear of repetitively feeling shamefully inadequate lay behind such self-protections; I just wasn't sure how to 'go there' with him.

My supervisor patiently reminded me that analysis was a long road, that we were still in early stages. She observed that Alan's self-protections were keenly intellectualized, and that contempt could feel 'yucky' (a perfect word). Additionally, since Alan had grown up in such an affectively constrictive surround, analytic vulnerability (with a male especially) would now inevitably be fraught with risk. In her view, the simple fact that Alan was still participating spoke well of our relationship.

Encouraged, I returned to the work, where 'glimmers' of affective vulnerability tantalized with hopes of deeper understanding. He told me about a painful depression during college, when he realized his childhood life was over for good. He had characteristically berated himself for an inability to 'pull himself out' of it. I wondered if this suffering was related to his mis-attuned, chaotic surround. He reiterated that his parents had good intentions and huge hearts. I then wondered if he might be feeling some guilt for leaving home, perhaps 'abandoning' his parents. He said maybe (!) ... before switching into self-criticism over his online shenanigans. I wanted to convey to him how deeply I sensed his dilemma, a vulnerability over thwarted *relational* needs he was never allowed to have. I couldn't.

I privately wondered if, as some of my recovery colleagues would say, a treatment program was needed, that he was not analyzable while still in his (online) cups. The referring psychiatrist too, active within the treatment community, mentioned earlier that Alan required a 12-step program for compulsive sexuality. I feared said psychiatrist might disapprove of my 'going analytic' with Alan. Meanwhile, I was discovering that there seemed to be no way of 'landing' in a position or analytic stance with this patient that might empathically survey or hold in mind some cohesive collage of his feeling-states in total. His fretful detours or oscillations jarred us into disparately divisive feeling-states, uncommunicative with one another as he and I struggled to find common ground: an intersubjective Tower of Babel.

Only after we had resolved the impasse described below did I see how impossible—at this point, at least—was the patient's holistic self-integration, which I hoped I could facilitate (a bit impatiently, like Alan), even as our analytic project included the spurned invitation of historically forbidden affect: this was the Brandchaftian 'operating system' instilled in him at an early age, now slowly in my own awareness as an intimidating (perhaps insurmountable?) system.

Alan then reported his porn use had metastasized; he now feared he was a full-fledged sex addict, though he was sure he wasn't. To soothe *this* anxiety, he'd resumed contact with Wendy after taking a break, which provoked a blast of self-loathing, and asking me if we were getting anywhere. I wondered again if it was worth giving Al-anon a try.

He bristled, 'I told you, that's for people who are really fucked-up.'

Had I bet on the wrong horse with Dr. Brandchaft? Maybe this patient needed something more directive, a 'tough' recovery philosophy. Was I detecting a naïve softness within my own beloved theory—as if this good theoretical 'father' were himself misattuned, leaving me to flounder? Yet who was I to question a 'legend'? On the other hand, Brandchaft only alluded to addictive processes; I wondered how *he'd* try a sustained empathic inquiry with Alan. *Put your money where your mouth is, Bernie!*

Our disjunction blossomed into impasse after Alan received an angry email from Wendy; tired of his ambivalence (he decided to take a break again), she blasted him a 'Dear John' message: 'liar,' 'wishy-washy' were some of the milder sobriquets. Karen was Mary Poppins in comparison.

He related this to me while looking pale and disheveled. Alarmed, I decided to try an intervention my own analyst had once employed to good effect. A bit impulsive, but I had to do *something*.

I said, after he'd railed on himself a bit, 'Look, I think what you're really seeking is closeness and validation and support.'

'That's what got me into trouble,' he said.

'It's *human*,' I said. He paused. I said I understood that the *what* of his interactions with Wendy were frustrating, but maybe there was an alternative outlet since the *why* (his need for appreciation and emotional safety) was so essential. Then, taking a breath, I said, 'Maybe there's more *I* can do to help you.'

He sat there, blank as a board.

I said, 'Maybe sex is a bit of a red herring here.'

'I know, it's really a problem.'

'That's not what I ...' I paused. 'You have very normal needs for closeness and understanding.' Silence. I hesitated, then: 'I'm saying ... maybe you could start bringing some of those needs and feelings *to me.*'

He looked puzzled. 'I thought that's what I was doing.'

'Well, sure, I just, er, hate to see you suffering and ... ' *quit while you're ahead* ' ... maybe there's more I can do. Like we could talk about your hopes and wants together, see where that gets us.'

He paused, confused. 'You think I'm *not* doing that?'

Crap. 'Look ... this is a safe place, I hope.'

'Obviously, or I wouldn't be coming.'

'None of this is meant as criticism.'

'I don't see your point,' he said, now irritated. 'It sounds like you're not happy about something,' he said, 'like maybe I'm off track, but you're not coming out and saying it.'

'You're not off track,' I blurted, though by now the whole session was off track.

His voice rose with agitation. 'I see you three times a week, I tell the truth, I tell you how hard this is, I'm freaked out ... ' He hesitated, as if fatigued. 'Forget it,' he snapped, squinting now, as if trapped in a vice. 'I'm tired, I had a rough night. Sorry.'

He kept his eyes shut, arms folded in front of him. We sat in a tense and brooding silence. He cancelled his next couple of sessions.

A Moment of Clarity

I uncomfortably reflected on the fact that somehow, in this last session, I had become what I had dreaded and tried to *avoid* becoming: a critical, demanding father—at the very moment I was hoping to provide a more expansive experience. Where had I gone wrong?

I began, via my own analysis, to recognize that the high expectations I placed on myself for perfection, even now as a candidate and relatively new analyst, themselves an antidote to repetitive shame. I had unwittingly clung to the old idea that 'doing it right' would immunize me against criticism or contempt. I now saw this as a defense against perceived inadequacy. Here hiding in plain sight was one of *my* immutable beliefs: *Do it right or else!* That 'or else' implied abandonment. No wonder treatment with Alan often felt pressurized, tying my hands in unforeseen ways.

I found in my own analysis, with its newfound emotional flexibility and 'permission' (see Orange, 2008), an opportunity to explore previously shunted feelings of shame and anger, both with and *at* my analyst (transferentially). Painful early experiences were now *contextualized*, helping me understand how caregivers' abandonments led organically to my own accommodations– *as a matter of survival.*

In other words, Brandchaft was a kind of map, analysis the journey itself.

This was a relief. I had long felt shame about accommodation itself, or 'people-pleasing,' a term bandied about in recovery circles. But I now viewed it as deriving from contextually repetitive derailments, rather than 'selfish' or 'needy,' as caregivers—and, later, caregiver-figures—implied for their own self-protection.

This led me to further reflect upon my work with Alan; perhaps some of his defensive processes (especially contempt and antidote-seeking) were triggering *my* anxiety, shame and even anger, with paternal-esque implications of my own 'failure' or inadequacy, frustrating hopes of being a good-enough analyst. *Let me be empathic here, would you?* Alan and I had unwittingly co-created a mutually reinforcing defensive process leading to stalemate. I took a look at my own self-ideals, accept the inevitability of mis-steps, noting the pervasive power of prereflective affect.

My own fallibility (Orange, 1995) now appeared inevitable, as did my need for assistance and support for this difficult work—as opposed to pass/fail requirements to be 'figured out' on my own, even with patients! Here was a dyadically disavowed vulnerability. Our striving for a closed-system *in*fallibility only constricted us.

Gradually I came to believe that trauma-rooted organizing was *intersubjectively generated* archaically and thus, hopefully, mitigated (Orange, 2008); to take *sole* responsibility for analytic work (as patient and analyst) was the accommodative legacy of a noxious caregiver system.

This clarified interlocking transferential configurations between me and Alan, confirming Brandchaft's observation that both participants 'are vulnerable ... to the activation of their respective developmental traumatic systems' (2010, p. 208). Alan's wariness of vulnerability and anxious interrogations stirred my own, especially when I hoped for signs of 'progress' with one of my first analysands, eagerly welcomed and anticipated.

My own analysis helped me stay mindful of a temptation to dissociate from stinging feelings, rather than become curious about what was might be going on here. It had after all appeared dangerous to 'mess up.' Alan was probably experiencing something similar. *Analyst, heal thyself.*

I also imagined that some of my silent confusion and hesitancy in the consulting room, stemming from the uncertainty just described, were likely interpreted by Alan as a sign *he'd* done something 'wrong,' paralleling perhaps his mother's withdrawals. I remembered his asking me early in treatment if I found him 'difficult'—which I now heard as shame. My comments about working more closely together probably sounded paternalistic, like criticism, amplifying anxiety and discouraging to the efforts he made, which

I to a degree overlooked (anxiety is befogging). How awkward this process, for someone with such manly ideals to accommodate, where any speck of daylight between his ideals and performance provoked terror of attack or disappointment. Yet this was asymmetrically occurring on both sides of the dyad.

I began to understand what Orange (2008) meant when she said, regarding dyadic shame, that it begins to act like 'an allergic reaction in the other, and the reactions themselves generate more and more difficulty' (p. 92). The blindness to my own archaic shame had obscured the potential insights offered by my own transferences.

Perhaps I had been a bit cowed by the terror behind the rigidity of his self-ideals, presented as inarguable due to the anxiety they buttressed. I also had overestimated the seductions of the intellect, as if theoretical understanding alone could save us from the uncertainties and *angst* of finitude, our human vulnerability. The intellectual mind sees the delineation of affectivity as *conceptual* rather than lived; Brandchaft's theory is easier to grasp than it is to dyadically apply, let alone experience. Alan might need help, perhaps with a dash of our emergent humor and playfulness, in recognizing and validating his own self-delineation (see Trop & Stolorow, 1992), bound as it was in the foregrounding of others. (Thus, my perceived criticism, in the above transaction, must have been terrifying for him.)

It might also help to mirror the strengths I genuinely observed—tolerating his wife's drinking, his principles of loyalty and self-sacrifice, exaggerated to me but vital to him for survival.

In a way, we were replicating our respective early surrounds which themselves disallowed authentic self-experience, given the required slavishness to immutable truths and caregivers' fragility. This was a recent discovery of mine as a *patient*, which led to a greater flexibility as an analyst, in understanding what was so dangerous for Alan.

The terror of differentiating from a father who both oppressed and protected him, I began to see, led Alan to (abrasively at times) see emotionality itself as a weakness. Alan had mentioned that his father also looked askance at *therapy*, leading to even more shame in his current 'straying' from paternalistic ideals, as fundamental differentiation remained dangerous. In this sense, *merely showing up* was momentous. Alan had *never* experienced mirroring with an empathic male; he probably didn't know what to make of me. It would take time to acclimate and work through the danger and risk of non-accommodative selfhood. His willingness to even make the attempt warranted recognition.

Analysis is often grueling. Working with unconscious accommodation is difficult; relational trauma has a much more pervasively destructive impact than I realized. It was a bittersweet awakening, and a heightened value of analysis' possibilities. Relational trauma widens the relational divide; it is relational understanding that begins to heal this gap, ease the either/or. It was ok for both Alan and I to muddle along as best we could. I looked forward to addressing our heated interaction soon as he returned—though Alan, being Alan, wanted to pretend it never happened.

***

I did gently insist, however, that we give it a passing mention, at which point he said he had felt 'a little criticized' the last time; he was receptive to my sharing my own conflict between wanting to be helpful without placing more demands on him—the very last thing he needed. He laughed, then reiterated he was doing the best he could—which I acknowledged, in a way that relaxed him.

He told me he and Wendy had made nice, followed by her insisting on a hotel rendezvous. I saw a flash of terror in his eyes—perhaps, I wondered aloud, a fear or contempt of his own desire to see her privately? A vexing, bland expression asserted itself before he said, 'Talk talk talk, that's all we ever do … ' He sighed, arms crossed.

I sat back a moment, stung (had I moved too fast?)—but then I paused, and leaned forward. 'So, you're saying … all we really do is talk, which gets us nowhere.' He nodded. I said, 'Same shit, different day.' Another nod. I went on: 'You come here time after time, paying your money, driving through traffic, frustrated … ' He was about to speak; I kept going. 'You pay, you come back, pay again, hoping things will get better, but they don't, you want Karen to stop, she doesn't, you want to forget about it, you can't, you try and try, and all we do is talk and it's all so *fucking frustrating!*'

I hesitated … wondering if I'd gone too far.

He broke into the widest grin I'd ever seen.

'I didn't know you could swear,' he said.

'Oh … well I—'

'No, it's *good*. I mean … you get it.' He paused, a lighter energy suddenly in the room. He leaned back. 'Feel free to swear more.'

'Well,' I said pleasantly. 'Fuckin' A.'

It occurred to me in that moment that I was Darren *as* analyst, not Darren *and* analyst.

This ice-breaking moment led to better understanding. His transference to me included my power to support *or destroy* (if I disapproved) his tender hopes of expansiveness—if, for example, I became a father reflecting his son's inarguable 'weakness.' He walked the knife edge, vigilantly searching for repetitive stirrings that provoked terror of falling into exile. Cybersex seduced him into thinking it could and *would* soothe this stress precisely, while reinforcing exile on the other end.

My recognizing his distinctive hopes and fears helped him—slowly, painstakingly—tolerate such uncomfortable feeling states, as I validated his needs and recognized his strengths within the context of a yearning for connection, a safer attachment. His analytic experience founded the 'truth' of his specific self-experience. When he moved away or threw up walls, I was able to mention it with a spirit of play or humor, or wait until the right moment without seeing this *automatically* as a mistake on my part, due to my own analytic 'weakness'. We'd made a sort of beginning.

Conclusion

Alan and I stumbled upon a 'moment of meeting' (Sander, 1992) via a conjunction of frustration beneath our disjunctive viewpoints. My outburst was an expression of frustration toward *dyadic* 'killer' organizing that had us both in its grip; we became siblings in repetitive deflation. My own analysis helped me shed the somewhat neutering 'professional' demeanor, my idea of how an analyst ought to be (according to my reading of the 'perfectly presented' Brandchaft, and other eloquent theorizing), allowing a more spontaneous irreverence that brought fresh air into the room. I could get 'down and dirty' with Alan via profanity, which as an ex-New Yorker came naturally to me. This helped him be ok with his own visceral desires and hurts, as I too saw the metaphorical monsters under the bed: unswayable proof of his unworthiness, an unending future that repeated a past of fraught isolation and Sisyphean demands.

Perhaps the question then is not 'how do we work with unconscious accommodation' but how does it work *us,* dyadically? Or, 'what conscious and unconscious organizing *of our own* is likely to be activated within this specific dyad?' In a strange way, the more similar the organizing, the greater the chance of retraumatization. As Brandchaft implied (2010, p. 198), a dyad's intersubjectivity includes the analyst's own developmental hopes (analytic 'goals') and repetitive fears, the latter likely to be triggered at some point or another.

Ironic, in a way, how Brandchaft's theory of intersubjectivity becomes, in the end, an example of the intersubjectivity of (applied) theory.

What I take from all this is that the analytic emancipations he spoke about comes with the risk of (asymmetrical) re-traumatization for both, *if* the work is proceeding. If we after all are asking our patients to re-visit painful, disavowed experiences, our own parallel analogues will also (as a kind of pre-condition) be 'on the table' for some potentially difficult self-reflection or re-experiencing.

For so many of our patients, *any* step beyond their narrow developmental relational 'horizon' (Stolorow, Atwood & Orange, 2002) is so frighteningly unknown and unimaginable, that in our empathic immersion or introspection we are likely to find a re-experiencing of our own unsayable darkness—throwing shadow on the outcome of analysis, as it is not a guarantee we can help our patients through their own darknesses; we are not *literal* caregivers after all.

So many of our patients are seeking someone to take that leap into the unspeakable unknown *with them*, stay *with them* rather than flee like everyone else. (See Stolorow on emotional dwelling (2013).) A *cordon sanitaire* set of rules or elegant theoretical 'truths' does not in the end do the trick, as our re-experiencing frightening voids provokes us in ways unknowable at the start. Stepping into our patients' experiential worlds implies, at times, the risk of again facing psychic terror; accepting this seems the surest way of proceeding, even as we cannot accept what remains unforeseen.

Brandchaft seems to know this: re-reading his work, I sense his commitment and generosity in stepping forward for his patients time and again, emerging with much to report to those of us stepping behind him. With his lucid eloquence and analytic wisdom, he makes it look easy. The great ones often do.

References

Alcoholics Anonymous (2001). *New York: A.A.* World Services, Inc.

Atwood, G.E. (2012). *The abyss of madness.* New York: Routledge.

Brandchaft, B. (2010). Systems of pathological accommodation in psychoanalysis. In B. Brandchaft, S. Doctors, & D. Sorter, *Toward an emancipatory psychoanalysis: Brandchaft's intersubjective vision* (pp. 193–220). New York: Routledge.

Jones, D.B. (2009). Addiction and pathological accommodation: An intersubjective look at impediments to the utilization of Alcoholics Anonymous. *International Journal of Psychoanalytic Self Psychology,* 4: 212–234.

Orange, D.M. (1995). *Emotional understanding.* New York: Guilford Press.

Orange, D.M. (2008). Whose shame is it anyway?: Lifeworlds of humiliation and systems of restoration (Or 'The analyst's shame'). *Contemporary Psychoanalysis,* 44: 83–100.

Sander, L.W. (1992). Countertransference. *International Journal of Psychoanalysis,* 73: 582–584.

Stolorow, R.D. (1999). Antidotes, enactments, rituals, and the dance of reassurance: Comments on the case of Joanna Churchill & Alan Kindler. *Progress in Self-Psychology,* 15: 229–232.

Stolorow, R.D. (2007). *Trauma and human existence.* New York: The Analytic Press.

Stolorow, R.D. (2011, October 18). Trauma and the hourglass of time [blog post]. Retrieved from www.psychologytoday.com/blog/feeling-relating-existing/201110/trauma-and-the-hourglass-time.

Stolorow, R.D. (2013, August 10). Undergoing the situation [blog post]. Retrieved from: www.psychologytoday.com/blog/feeling-relating-existing/201308/undergoing-the-situation.

Stolorow, R.D. & Atwood, G.E. (1992). *Contexts of being: The intersubjective foundations of psychological life.* Hillsdale, NJ: The Analytic Press.

Stolorow, R.D., Atwood, G.E., & Orange, D.M. (2002). *Worlds of experience: Inter-weaving philosophical and clinical dimensions in psychoanalysis.* New York: Basic Books.

Stolorow, R.D., Brandchaft, B., & Atwood, G.E. (1987). *Psychoanalytic treatment: An intersubjective approach.* Hillsdale NJ: The Analytic Press.

Trop, J.L. & Stolorow, R.D. (1992). Defense analysis in self psychology: A developmental view. *Psychoanalytic Dialogues,* 2: 427–442.

Chapter 6

A Comedy of Terrors

Franz Kafka and a Vexing Case of
Porn Addiction

Introduction

The sociocultural influence of Franz Kafka is hard to overestimate, the term *Kafkaesque* long established in our lexicon, still applicable to (among other things) our labyrinthine immigration and healthcare systems. Kafka's totemic influence on literature has also been noted by (among others) Milan Kundera (1988) and Gabriel Garcia Marquez (Jordison, 2017), who cite Kafka as arguably the precursor to magic realism.

There is also a place for him in analytic thinking, as Ogden (2009), Schafer (1997), and Kohut (1975) have shown. What I attempt in this chapter is to further illustrate the clinical usefulness of Kafka's writing, with its metaphors made useful for the intersubjective confusions of working with addicted patients. Such patients' relational contexts are often characterized by Brandchaftean (2010) accommodation, as well as isolated-mind, Cartesian thinking (Stolorow & Atwood, 1992), and confusing conceptualizations. The epistemic tyranny of patients' relational systems results in a series of desires leading nowhere but futility, and the deflation of subjective agency into a passivity sometimes vexing for the analyst. Welcome to the *Kafkaesque.*

I employ herein a case study to illustrate the relevance of Kafka's fiction and psychobiography, all characterized by maze-like psychic ensnarements. Kafka's minutely-crafted comic nightmares give form to often puzzling clinical absurdities. My patient James was much like Josef K. in *The Trial* (1946), arrested without knowing the charges; soon James' analyst, too, was guilty by association, our process sputtering. Embracing the futility of my approach proved the only viable solution, to help me understand his stuckness and our predicament; it was our mutual 'guilt' in the end that, in a twist worthy of Kafka, got us in the clear.

In the Maze

I have found that the *Kafkan* world, sprawling with a confusion and despair eerily normalized, often belies a tenderness at the heart of the author's

DOI: 10.4324/9781003266358-7

sensibility. The sophisticated literary mythos of Franz Kafka has led, in my own biographical research, to the early worldhood of a precocious yet abandoned gifted child (Miller, 1998), condemning himself for the 'selfishness' of needs burdensome *to others*. Young Franz's reliance, on caregivers who found him demanding, led to his perceiving as 'toxic' his most tender foundational strivings.

In such a caregiving scenario (commonly observed in my practice), the child's pursuit of love, recognition, or fulfillment leads nowhere but abuse or neglect, unrecognized and interpreted by the child as a shameful 'verdict': a labyrinth of foreclosure wherein the child (or, later, the adult patient's) vulnerability is left to take the blame entirely.

This held true for James, a man whose self-hatred fueled an addiction to pornography, itself perpetuating a lacerating shame further soothed by the addiction itself, a circularity leading nowhere except a plaguing inadequacy he then again had to soothe … all foreclosing the analytic relationality I hoped to engender.

My early efforts were met with a brick wall. This resulted in cul-de-sacs provoking self-doubts of my own, an entrapping quest for redemption, both of us increasingly guilty of some unnamable crime.

A belated self-recognition on my part—namely, a re-imagining of such a labyrinthine case involving my own archaic contributions and unseen emotional analogues, together with a surprising turn of personal events, (replace dash with comma please) provided the golden thread. I recognized the traumatized child in him, after contacting some overwhelming *Kafkaesque* trauma of my own, both of us loosening our grip on unseen yet somehow gripping antidotal illusions.

A Life Sentence

For all of the voluminous writings about Kafka, about the sociopolitical heft of his metaphors and narratives, we find at the center of the work—in *The Metamorphosis* (1948) especially, perhaps Kafka's finest work—a raw, human yearning for belonging. Kafka's characters pursue what is so commonly craved: a semblance of familial love, actual (in *Metamorphosis*) or symbolic (in *The Trial*). Slowly his protagonists are diligently deflated to death, in both tales.

In *Metamorphosis*, the earnest, hard-working Gregor Samsa seeks to do right by his family, hoping to financially support them even after his transformation into a giant cockroach. Gregor wakes in verminous embodiment, before ascertaining how he might make it to work on time, a life of accommodation implied in a few darkly satirical strokes of the pen. (Anecdote has it that when Kafka read the opening of *The Trial* aloud to friends, everyone laughed, including the author (Kundera, 1988).)

Meanwhile Gregor's family, drawn with bleak, straight-faced irony, coolly distance themselves from Gregor, exiling and eventually destroying him. The disparity between Gregor's earnestness and his family's indifference leads to his absurdly literal extinction.

The chief irony at work here in my reading is that the attitude of the family towards Gregor, their indifference, is even more monstrous than the metamorphosis itself. They regard Gregor with contempt and themselves with self-pity (echoed in Kafka's epistolary descriptions of his father). Gregor seems to view his transformation with all the seriousness of a head cold, as he scurries in and out of his bedroom, climbing the walls restlessly, his sticky legs holding him aloft, while he eats little or nothing, hiding beneath the couch in an attempt to maintain familial semblance without repelling them. Yet authentic family unity may, we slowly sense, have long been illusory; his family finds him repulsive, especially now that he cannot earn his keep. (In his *Letter*, Kafka refers to himself and his father as 'vermin' (1966, p. 107).)

The irony is further twisted by the fact that Gregor can hear but cannot speak, his voice transformed into an insect-like screech. The family is meanwhile unaware that he can hear every word of their derision and self-pity.

The father ultimately loses his patience with Gregor's hovering, pelting his son with hurled apples, wounding Gregor and driving him into his room once and for all. Gregor, in solitary confinement, his room now utilized as the family's storage closet, is overwhelmed with injury and despair, collapsing with a final breath. His body is disposed of by a charwoman—who is then fired. The family goes for an outing at the end, enjoying the fine weather, their daughter basking in youthful beauty. It is implied they are happier without him.

Alongside this sunny narrative is *The Trial* (1946), also told with calm equanimity. We begin with Josef K.'s arrest one morning in bed, for unstated reasons. The increasingly exasperated K. spends the entire novel (I almost typed 'treatment') seeking the actual charges, and how to vindicate himself— all, of course, in vain. Everyone seems to know about his case, surprised at his useless search for answers. Scenes often take place in surreal spaces such as bedrooms transformed into courtrooms, the domestic and the bureaucratic conflated. The Court is everywhere and nowhere all at once, like the Law itself: a most menacing caregiver-system. (I also think of the case of Breonna Taylor, killed in her own home by police for no real reason.)

Along the way Josef has a few erotic encounters, always interrupted. It is even implied his darkly attractive femme fatale neighbor is his informer. At story's end, K. is assassinated by knife at midnight, by two anonymous officials, 'like a dog! ... as if the shame of it should outlive him (2005, Kindle Location 3055),' a somewhat tacked-on ending; the novel was never fully completed to Kafka's satisfaction, as tuberculosis fatally intervened.

What I wish to emphasize via both tales is the bleakly ironic elusiveness of any sense of the 'why' of one's abuse, *deserved nonetheless*, as authoritative forces remain rigid, dominant, *familiar*. This is also a hallmark of

Kafka's childhood, under an inflexible monomaniacal father. The contemptuous, sarcastic Hermann Kafka appeared incapable of any tenderness at all toward Franz or the latter's creative pursuits, viewed by Hermann as a waste of time.

Kafka's *Letter to his Father* (1966) reveals his own tormenting ambivalence, toward a father he shunned while craving his approval, even as Franz knew such craving was fruitless, given his father's disappointment and Franz's own 'disloyalty' via his differentiation and the subsequently permanent disappointment of his father, stoking a Sisyphean self-contempt.

What surprised me upon re-reading this letter was Kafka's absolving (mostly) his father of any guilt or accountability, as they were both 'helpless' (p. 51) to change their dynamic, like two hapless children under God. Kafka is more ambivalent about his own guilt, almost as if the attempts to absolve Hermann quells his own mounting fury, possibly sinful. Such fury was likely dangerous for Kafka, as it made him more 'father-like.' Kafka's characters also dread burdening or offending others.

In the *Letter*, Kafka oscillates between a hot woundedness and the belief that Hermann could not help himself—as if, yet again, the true 'sin' is Kafka's anger at a man whose nature is clearly unchangeable. Again, longings for paternal love become seen as misguided. The *Letter* also implies they are quite similar, a chip off the old ice-block.

Such scenarios are also seen with patients, with the child/adult continuing to pursue a love that is hopeless (for instance an affair with a married person or 'emotionally unavailable' others), with desire increasingly burdensome on the other and again therefore 'wrong,' albeit inevitable. Relationality remains futile, even meaningless. This is why Kafka's *Letter* is so heartbreakingly astute, at times achingly humorous.

Such a *Kafkan* admixture of humor and tragedy are also found in the relational worlds of patients struggling with addiction (one of my specialties) and its 'Siamese twin,' reflexive accommodation. (What is an addiction after all but accommodation to tyrannical processes?) Often a patient's illusory hope is that one day, the addiction will vanish and/or a loving recognition long craved will be delivered, once somehow *earned*, in accordance with an inflexibly haunting self-ideal.

Consider James, a soft-spoken, pensive man in his late thirties, raised by a philandering, hapless father, and a self-pitying yet intensely critical mother (echoes of Hermann), both of whom overlooked their son's development entirely. James' differentiation was, in fact, ever an obstacle. They bestowed favor upon his beautiful, academically gifted older sister, who (as in *Metamorphosis*) saw her withdrawn brother as competition: two famished children vying for scraps.

James seemed at times a walking shadow, in the aftermath of unrecognized abuse. His father was thrown out of the house when James was young, later treating his son as a 'pal,' showing the boy pornographic magazines when

James was only ten or eleven. This would set in motion for James a perpetual confusion of identity, as he was similar to a man who repelled his family, which James wished to avoid even as he followed (to his horror) in his father's psychological footsteps.

His mother also shuffled him upon the playing board of her needs, venting her wrath on him (as a substitute for her husband perhaps), while treating him as a surrogate companion, sharing unwelcome details of her life, including her loneliness and the sexual failings of his father. All of this was painful, he told me—for *her*. (As his wife's verbal abuses only confirmed *her* suffering in his view, due to the certainty of his ineptitude.)

It took long, painstaking effort for him to connect the dots of his trampled subjectivity, his caregivers' eroticized intrusiveness, and his compulsivity—to say nothing of the wariness of intimacy with his wife, given how dangerous was vulnerability. Until then, his sexual impulses led nowhere but self-loathing, porn, and more self-loathing due to porn—the compulsive soothing/exacerbation cycle of his habit.

James for the longest time remained convinced of his own unworthiness, keeping the noxious system in working order. He was caught in ceaseless ritualizations with his wife, Karen, predicated on her verbal lashings of his trivial (to my ears) oversights. She sounded even more venomously critical than his mother. He would misplace a pen or, lose a sock in the laundry, resulting in explosive wrath.

'Your carelessness is killing us!' she would say.

He found such rage incomprehensible yet deserved, as when she grilled him to 'explain' his addiction in a rational way, another task he found shamefully impossible.

James' archaic mental or epistemic abuse (Brandchaft, 2010) had also gone unrecognized. He wondered why he stringently prioritized the needs of others, his 'co-dependence,' only that he could not seem to stop. This soon led us into the thicket, as we shall see, until neither of us could win for losing.

He often remarked, in response to my observing his suffering as disproportionate to his lashings, 'but that's not how *she* sees it.' This included his inability to defend himself from his wife's tirades, amplified by her (deserved) wrath upon her recent discovery, via rummaging through his browsing history, that he had returned to porn. This sealed his fate and destroyed all marital credibility.

This had also occurred ten years earlier, at the start of the marriage. Karen found his 'stash' of DVDs and, understandably upset, insisted that James attend Sex Addicts Anonymous meetings (SAA), a 12-step program. He complied for several years with the program's recommended abstinence from porn, despite occasional cravings, relapsing before contacting me, again in terror's grip. I once mentioned that any accountability on his part notwithstanding, addiction or compulsivity never occurs in a relational vacuum; marriage is a system.

Said James, 'But that's not how *she* sees it.'

I clenched my teeth a bit and moved ahead.

He dearly hoped I could 'motivate' him to attend SAA, lest she exile him (like Gregor) for good. At the same time, he dreaded giving up his habit, to his bewildered shame. He hoped I could 'get' him to stop craving what served, I surmised, as a buffer against her rage. ('But *she* sees it as justified,' he told me.)

One of the parallels with Kafka's fiction involves James' confusion over the source of such inflexibly authoritative demands. Was it Karen who was pushing perfectionism, or was the latter again his 'co-dependence'?

In either event I observed his unquestionable overburdening, in (again) managing an entire system (Brandchaft, 2010) while 'interiorizing' traumatic affect while *also* jumping through relational hoops. (I sensed both he and Karen could not help but repeat such cycles.) This also echoed, I was slow to see, the little psychotherapist (Atwood, 2015) scenario of my own upbringing.

James, meantime, hoped with my help to 'earn' the love and validation he thirsted for, even if he didn't really deserve it—a task I saw as impossible. I supposed that such a hope, as a lattice for his sagging tendrils of yearning, was better than no hope at all (i.e., despair.)

Yet I soon found myself frustrated, towards James and his wife, as both contributed to a cyclical chaos inflicting untold damage on the both of them, and possibly their young child (I privately surmised). James appeared unable to do much besides absorb Karen's roaring blows, as an abusive way of life was again normalized, leading (again) back to his salvation in late-night images. The system was shot through with inflamed reactivity, and it appeared my job was to douse the fire as unseen dynamics remain locked in place. All of this felt eerily, uncomfortably familiar.

James for instance, for the longest time, asked me for 12-step guidance, which I delivered—and which he failed to follow almost entirely. My familiarity with recovery was advertised on my website: the reason he sought me out in the first place. SAA had been helpful to him (sort of); he could not understand his resistance to it now. At first, I was confused by his frequently flat affect, until I understood how foreclosed was the expression of almost any of his subjective desire or pain, outside of quelling his spouse's wrath.

At the time, I myself was torn between the behavioral modality of recovery, so personally and professionally familiar, and a newly expansive interest in relational theory, particularly intersubjective-systems.

I was winding down my 'stint' as a rehab counselor, and starting my analytic candidacy. The rehab espoused a 12-step philosophy, by that point second nature to me; it had undoubtedly saved my life.

But ten years after putting 'the plug in the jug,' I was hungry for more, enthused about analytic thought (as described in Chapter 5). I found resonant the approaches of phenomenological contextualization, including Brandchaft's attuned descriptions of accommodative systems (such as James', clearly). But I stumbled over some of my own subjective uncertainties, resonant with archaic loyalties of old, in turning toward analytic thought and away from my recovery 'family,' which also as a rule cautioned against straying too far. Here is where I too began to resemble Josef K, guilty of unnamable transgression.

I realized this would not be an easy case, given James' keen ambivalence and longtime enslavement. Any whiff of dependence had always led to obligations he could not reasonably fulfill, which I saw as a danger for him even in our work and, less consciously, as a factor in my relationship with my recovery sponsor (more below). Easier, then, for both of us to acquiesce to 12-step guidance, more 'tried and true' than the complicated, analytic way of working—as if I had to choose only one.

The analytic perspective seemed to jockey for position with behavioral interventions. Yet even regarding recovery, James' 'higher power' was clearly his wife, and that was not changing anytime soon. His initial hope in fact was to accommodate her more smoothly. How then to proceed? My empathic investigations did not get us far either, so distrustful was James towards his own 'toxic' emotionality. Where was I going wrong? Uncertainty rippled throughout.

Also complicating matters were the strains of accommodative demands found in some 12-step groups or individuals, as Jones (2009) has outlined. I for instance had at this time chosen a sponsor who hewed a 'party line' in regard to 12-step principles he claimed—with initially comforting certainty— were indisputable. This included the supremacy of 12-step principles over psychotherapy, in his view. Here was a man I had come to trust over many years, who in some ways knew me better than my own father.

Thus, I first interpreted James' reluctance as an unwillingness to 'surrender' to a program. But, at the same time, the burgeoning analyst in me wondered, 'where does this get us?'

I might for instance, seizing upon the futility of the recovery approach, switch hats by deciding to 'get more empathic.' But upon attempting to explore his childhood, things turned foggy for him, as is sometimes the case when caregivers' needs are inflexibly foregrounded, the child fading into the background, as experience and subsequent memory lost distinction. This can fuel the grip of grand authoritative principles, binding children from 'on high,' as with Kafka's Court and James' caregivers.

James and I meanwhile fell into our own Kafkaesque ritualization. His anxious ambivalence evoked my uncertainties about what I was supposed to be doing according to … who or what? What was an efficient salve to his palpable wounding? His helplessness practically screamed, 'Save me!' But was the 'tough love' of recovery warranted, or further attempts at empathic investigation? Both went mostly nowhere.

James' agony filled the room until we were both on trial, each failing the other, circling around the unspoken problem, even hiding from it—like a frightened child (or insect) beneath the bed.

The Severed Worm

Kafka tells us what his writing is about, very plainly, in the *Letter to his Father* (1966).

This eloquent, tortured missive was meant for posthumous delivery to Hermann, but Julie again once more protected her husband, withholding it even after her son Franz was dead.

In it the beleaguered son states to his father, 'my writing was all about you' (1966, p. 71): a paternity serving as 'a terrible trial … in which you keep on claiming to be judge' (p. 53). One gets the impression that such trial was always in session, the author guilty prior to opening arguments.

For all his rage and disappointment, Franz clearly could not shake the conviction that this was simply his father's nature, like the scorpion in Aesop's fable. Franz, perceiving himself as the doomed frog, could not help but beckon the venomous father onto his back, for a poisoning he apparently had coming.

Such a withholding of caregiver provision, I often observe, leads to the soothing provisions of compulsive activity later on, such fleeting warmth strangely *more self-restorative* (Stolorow and Atwood, 2014) than any experience with actual caregivers.

Even if the child later finds a more productive compulsivity (leading for instance to world-famous masterpieces), the psychic breach is never healed (Winnicott, 1971). Kafka claims his own work was ever overshadowed by a father stretching 'diagonally across [my] world,' a few spare 'regions … not covered by you or within your reach … these are not many and not very comforting' (1966, p. 107).

Kafka clearly needed to self-protect against painful early experience, dissociate we might say, which he perceives in the *Letter* as his own indifference or 'the sole defense against destruction of the nerves by fear and … guilt' (p. 71). A guilt perhaps over his own self-protective indifference: the agonies of a closed system. In this way, Kafka bore vexing resemblance to the man he silently condemned.

Alice Miller (1998) describes Kafka as a gifted child brutalized by his father, neglected by a mother kowtowing for survival. This left Franz at the mercy of the (also mistreated) household staff, who took out *their* frustration on the boy. Franz retreated into his imagination, drawing upon 'a child's intense and painful way of experiencing the world' (p. 240).

Hermann, a successful businessman, felt Franz's writing was useless, angry that his son refused to enter the family business. Miller senses Hermann made all of his children 'painfully aware of their weakness' (p. 283), especially Franz.

She recalls young Franz asking for a glass of water before bedtime, forced by Hermann to stand in the cold until he recanted his request. Franz 'undoubtedly didn't know what he was guilty of when he was beaten' (p. 287). We begin to see how the compliant child can only conclude their needs are dangerous. Kafka in adulthood remained borderline anorexic, hypochondriacal and prone to fad diets, as if his own physical boundaries were tenuous. When actual illness beset him, he saw it as both doom and blessing (Pawel, 1991); in the end he starved to death as he like Gregor lost his voice, due to his tuberculosis of the larynx.

Brandchaft (2010) describes how areas of selfhood can remain emaciated, due to a systemic undermining of fundamental differentiation. Miller in turn observes that a gifted child—and later in this case a most influential writer— cannot articulate his pain or longings because 'it would destroy him' (1998, p. 247). Children can recover from trauma, if contextually recognized or existentially seen (Stolorow, 2015), as for instance in psychoanalysis. What is initially soul-murdering is the prohibition of any affectivity threatening the system's *apparatchiks,* who find the child guilty day after day. This reinforces authoritative truths and subsequent self-ideals as *a priori.* Miller (1998) also notes the difficulty of such cases for archaically neglected analysts, who may need to distance themselves from their own analogous, prereflective pain.

A psychic torn-ness, the child pulling away from their own foundational strivings, is implicitly illustrated the *Letter,* the author referencing his rigorous creative pursuits as a paternally-unblemished 'region … slightly reminiscent of the worm that, when a foot treads on its tail end, breaks loose with its front part and drags itself aside' (Kafka, 1953/1966, p. 71). A 'worm' that, we may note, can never again be made whole, even for a writer as gifted as Franz Kafka.

Written on the Flesh

James' anguish often reminded me of Kafka's short story *In the Penal Colony* (1948/1975), about an enormous, clanking torture machine that inscribes the prisoner's crime into his flesh with a harrow of needles. I recall spotting James one morning as he climbed the stairs to my office, trudging heavily, with the air of the shunned, as if the word 'loser' had been carved into his skin.

Meanwhile our own dyadic trudge began to stall. He requested, and I dolefully provided, recommendations on SAA literature, meetings, and finding a sponsor. I discussed powerlessness and unmanageability. James remained mostly lifeless, bashing himself for not 'doing what I promised.' I would wonder aloud what was getting in the way. A guilty silence ensued. *Let's try something else,* I told myself. But for some unknown reason, I couldn't!

Meanwhile Karen blasted him with such unwarranted fury that I at times suppressed a laugh of astonishment. She would use a meat thermometer to make sure he had cooked dinner correctly, throwing the steak in the trash if it were off by a few degrees: There was also hell to pay if he washed the clothes at the improper setting, or used too much detergent, failures deserving the death penalty. The essential sin in each case was his causing her misery, which he failed to mitigate.

Soon I too felt handcuffed. His self-hatred appeared genuine, towards his own indisputable wretchedness. Was I adding to his misery, in not getting us on surer footing?

I occasionally, gently, wondered if he might suggest to Karen that her berating was taking a toll. (His young daughter also got upset when Karen screamed, but I stepped lightly there.) 'She thinks I deserve it,' he said. 'I can't keep up with her list.'

'Maybe it's impossible,' I said once.

'She doesn't see it that way.'

'How do you see it?'

James paused. 'I just really need stop getting her so mad.' And then an awkward silence.

I found him to be most intelligent, sincere, and undeserving of his early, abusive conditioning. Yet I grew irritated that he just 'took it' in regard to Karen, without pushing back, also happening with a callous supervisor at his work. His listlessness redefined passivity, as he appeared confused about the point of my empathic curiosity, since we were dwelling on the anxiety or pain 'getting in the way' of his performance. He was utterly unable to refrain from devaluing and distancing from his own self-experience.

He once told me he snored at night, to Karen's further agitation; she banished him to the worn couch, which he shared with the family's ornery, one-eyed cat. He once memorably stated, 'Well, another sleepless night on the couch with Jinxy. She pee'd on the blanket again.' Somehow this encapsulated our situation.

Once I laughed in disbelief at his report of Karen and her volcanic ire over, well, nothing (to my ears.) He seemed embarrassed; I feared I had mocked him, and told myself to zip it.

He said, 'I'm sure it sounds ridiculous.' And then another awkward silence.

I asked on one occasion if my 12-step suggestions were helping.

He said, 'Sure, just for some reason I don't want to do it!'

I speculated that maybe his life was full of people telling him what to do.

He said, 'Or maybe I'm not good at listening.'

'Maybe porn is keeping you sane.'

'But if *she* finds out … '

I hesitated, deflated. There was frustration there, and a fear of his noticing it, as with his boss, wife, and mother.

I also struggled with a personal trial of my own. At that time my recovery sponsor tended, as indicated earlier, to disparage the usefulness of therapy in treating addiction. He strongly believed only the 12-step approach was effective, that therapeutic attunement was almost always pointless.

'Self-knowledge and insight avail us nothing,' he often repeated.

I often thought of this when sitting with James, wondering if we were both spinning our wheels. Yet Brandchaftian tendencies here were practically shouting; surely the analytic view had merit. Perhaps the theory was on target, though I was not. Or was James simply not 'surrendering'? Or was he 'unanalyzable'? But such thoughts were a no-no in relational theory.

Then James reported viewing pornography at work, during lunchtime, against company policy. He was terrified of being found out. He spoke of being mistreated there as well, but feared repercussions for speaking up against a domineering boss. Karen had long said his one saving grace was his salary, which freed her to pursue an acting career; he dare not put that in jeopardy! Still, porn remained a tempting if toxic antidote. He must have noticed my concern, as he dramatically committed to attending an SAA meeting, but later told me he failed to attend, due to Karen's to-do list.

One day he told me Karen was dissatisfied, not seeing any therapeutic 'progress.' He was behind on his chores and could not explain to her his porn addiction, in a way she found logical. He feared she would insist he find another therapist (which sometimes happens in addiction cases), as he mightily struggled to keep up with washing the car, cleaning out the garage, and taking Jinxy to the vet (he had the scratches to prove it). He did find helpful my speculations about Karen's own early trauma, the agony of her paternal abandonment expressed in her rages perhaps. But Karen could not acknowledge or adjust her contributions, and refused couples counseling, the burden remaining on him as *he* after all was the porn addict. Compliance remained mandatory, the whole system on lockdown.

I had by that point come to see James as a kind of little brother, abused as my actual younger brother had been, in our chaotically addictive family system—receiving as the youngest the trailing brunt of my parents' rage and neglect. I occasionally feared I had not done enough to protect him—had in fact mistreated him at times, out of my own frustration.

Yet James was also repetitively father-like for me, in his passivity in the face of an addiction (or compulsivity) tearing him and his family apart. Thus, my empathy vied with irritation, as I struggled with a confusing torn-ness of my own.

One day I suggested, more overtly than usual, that James tell Karen in his kind and inimitable way to back off on the idea of switching therapists. Change takes time, I said, and we had built a nice rapport.

He said, irritated, 'You know you sit here and say that, but I'm the one who has to deal with her at home.'

I looked at him, astonished.

Suddenly I saw how Karen's bullying had so repelled me that I backed away rather than lean into his experience.

Here he started to apologize, but I encouraged him to say more. He quietly related the constant pressure to please others, including me, for which he again blamed his 'codependence.' How terribly unsafe it was for him to risk another's disappointment! He destroyed himself to mitigate an even more unthinkable catastrophe: being proven a useless piece of garbage in the eyes of a loved one. By staying with Karen, his 'criminal case' remained on appeal, as he sought a strictly performative approach, the relational language of his worldhood. No wonder his own affectivity was ever devalued, *trashed,* keeping at bay the very 'weak' or burdensome emotionality he needed to understand his own experience. (I was, in other words, putting him in a bind without seeing it.)

He appeared relieved at my insistence of my contribution to our enact-ment, in giving him the task of standing up to Karen, from the sidelines ... much like his father, perhaps?

'I can see that,' he said, after a moment.

I observed that what he had received for so long was the very opposite of guidance.

I privately dwelled on the traps I had fallen into, organizing my supervisors and beloved theorists, as well as my recovery sponsor (and even my patient at times!), as fathers—expansive and then demanding, in line with archaic conditioning.

Slowly I saw I had nurtured the hope, perhaps the illusion, that in intersubjective-systems I had found a way *around* the oddly familiar dis-comfort evoked by James' suffering, a notion that theory might 'armor' me, allow *only* for insights that might soothe the dyad and lead to the promised land: the illusion in other words that I had finally escaped my father's house *for good.* In fact, dwelling *within* suffering, alongside the patient (Stolorow & Atwood, 2016), however uncomfortable or suffocating for the analyst, was what the theory called for, in order to make sense of it dialogically and allow relational ventilation.

I had fallen under the hypnotic tug of the familiar, in other words, in the transferential grip (Socarides & Stolorow, 1984) to *fully* and impossibly pro-tect James, much as James hoped to avoid retraumatization via a perfect compliance to Karen.

I at the same time (in line with paternal repetition) feared disappointing both James and my mentors and even my sponsor, as the patient feared dis-appointing me, leading us into guilty confusion, as a genuine rapport for-tunately developed. But even as warmth and humor emerged, we pursued mutually reinforcing mirages of self-protection. In a way James' resistance to 12-step (and his analyst) were admirable, as he otherwise showed zero rebel-lion. But rather than explore it, I sought to persuade him 'out of it'—as if encouraging Josef K. to respect the authority of the court.

Such familiarity led to a repetitive searching for suggestions we knew were (probably) useless, even as I hoped to magically unlock of James' resistance. Our stalled empathic inquiry made both of us anxious, as I myself struggled with an archaic anxiety to 'figure it out' and 'get it right,' ever the straight-A student. In other words, I sometimes asked more questions rather than stop and look into his anxiety (and mine, now mutually reinforcing).

Of course, none of this is black and white; some practical suggestions are useful to patients, and were to James—but only as a side attraction. The patient's subjectivity is what in the end holds center stage, both tempting and terrifying for archaically abandoned patients. Meanwhile, James and I remained mostly in the wings, in terms of emotionality, signaling to each other from afar and amidst catastrophe.

The real question was, how did James remain in such painful enslavement? What kept it going, and what was this like for him as a child and now, moment to moment? What would even a smidgeon of incremental freedom look like? And what was happening between us? Any 'answer' was an empathic process, leaning in rather than a detouring our asymmetrical agony.

This particular dyad in other words had come to resemble the torn halves of Kafka's wriggling worm: unconnected, disenjoined. Healing would be dialogic, not mechanical or performative, a collaborative outlining of the crushing 'boot' of unrecognized trauma, repeated at home, with a wife I privately resented and James pursued, in his hope of gleaning a crumb from her table, to stave off an affective famine destroying him from the inside out.

Finitude

Soon after James' pushback, I suggested that we forget about the literal compulsion and examine the affective function served by his compulsivity (Khantzian, 1995). James asked if this was 'allowed.' *May it please the court … I told him we had nothing to lose—and besides, this was all for* him.

This helped our cause immensely. The freer James spoke of his use of porn with lessened self-castigation, about the dark depths of its attractions in the midst of suffering, the easier it was for him to put it aside incrementally, until before long he had stopped entirely.

He would start sessions by reporting another few days of abstinence, a sly twinkle of pride in his eyes. He also found Karen's behavior even more painful, and on occasion quietly, tentatively asked her to stop. Sometimes it worked, sometimes she could not stop herself, exploding furiously … leading me to ask him if his was the only compulsion in the picture. Over time, he was able to assert his own psychic space, protect himself in ever incremental ways. This both calmed and exacerbated Karen's anger. But I became more understanding of his dilemma, facilitating an expansive relational space.

Something else happened around this time I wish to touch on, an unexpected event in my personal life, inadvertently loosening my own shackling.

One day I learned my father had died, after a long battle with heart disease, alcoholism, and a generally self-destructive lifestyle.

Though there is not sufficient space to explore it here, I find it pertinent to touch upon amidst this chapter's paternal themes. My father's death put a capstone on a lifetime of paternal absence, a final abandonment after, I soon recognized, bottomless disappointment—in ways that paralleled Hermann Kafka's influence on his son, and on James via his own caregivers. I grieved the father lost and, even more so, the one never found, with surprising intensity. It starkly revealed how life was more finite than I had acknowledged, but also that I had chosen a different path than him, in getting sober and staying more attuned to loved ones. I was *not* him, in other words, in a way both vindicating and bittersweet.

It also dissolved the illusion of finding the long-sought paternal recognition I sought, at least in regard to the transferential quagmire with my sponsor. Helpful as he had been in early going, I simply at this point needed something different. We parted ways, much to his surprise, I think.

Yet I came to see the absurdity of my own organization, in trying to stave off the disappointment of others at my own developmental expense, which helped silence the various clinical father figures arguing in my ear. ('Try 12-step!' 'That's not analytic!') In short, you can't please everyone. What mattered was helping the person in front of me, along intersubjectively specific lines.

The work with James deepened. I grieve my paternal losses still. Such is the sobering, melancholy touch of finitude.

***

James found, on his own, a recovery meeting he enjoyed and attended regularly. He even resumed working again on a screenplay idea that showed great promise, a science-fiction story about a planet of workers enslaved by a giant corporation. We had fun talking about rebellion and revenge.

He also provided for me a description of porn's pernicious pull, starting in early adolescence: an initially wondrous warm feeling 'filling me up,' belying the aching emptiness he must otherwise have carried. This conferred a fleeting yet vivid sense of the goodness of his own yearnings, with a yearning to be seen as good. Porn provided such euphoric expansiveness, at first. As with an abusive caregiver, the glimmer of fulfilment was soon followed by slavish demands. (Again, as with Gregor's absurd compliance post-transformation, the enslavements of addiction are a perfect fit within a Brandchaftean system.)

Such yearnings were of course then sexualized (they must after all go *somewhere*)—after a lifetime of sexualized intrusion, i.e., his mother's unboundaried frankness, his father's sharing porn. In fact, James' entire surround tended to eroticize longings as a means of camouflaging *caregivers'* archaically derailed recognition, as James symbolically learned the family language. But an abstinence from pornography freed him to pursue some of his desires relationally, with his analyst for instance, easing the need for his compulsively secret life to carry the load.

Porn became envisioned by both of us as a relief from the performative pressures James faced with every tick of the clock, at work, home, even with his mother, who continued to talk his ear off several times a week. Porn was also antidotal protection from sex with a woman he feared and knew he had disappointed, with whom any protest was dangerous since (like Gregor) he had long been deprived a voice, even as his distance continued to disappoint her.

Such deprivation had been menacingly literal. He told me he once as a youngster 'sassed' his mother, in the way a young boy might. His mother was instantly furious, grabbing him by the throat and pinning him to the wall, until he gasped and feared for his life. Finally, she released him, his eyes swimming, while his fear-stricken father stood by, watching. *Better you than me, kid.*

No wonder he anguished when I asked him to 'speak up'! Safer to find crumbs of vitalizing affirmation in pictures of topless women (his predilection) from cheaply printed magazines: a maternal 'provision' far safer (however fleeting) than his mother's abuse and father's absence, a narrow escape from the filicidal fate of Gregor Samsa.

A Stitch in Time

In the *Letter* we learn what plagued Kafka the most: his regret over his collapsed engagement to his fiancé, Felice Bauer.

It is probably not a surprise to learn that Kafka's romantic life was a tangled mess. One sees his eloquent ambivalence on display in his voluminous correspondence to Felice (Kafka, 1967/1973), whom he seduced and romanced from a comfortable distance, writing to her long letters several times a day.

So confusing were his stated intentions to marry (or not), that Felice brought in a friend to act as go-between. Franz took this friend, Grete Bloch, into his confidence—then fell in love with her as well. Grete extracted herself, as both women were now exasperated, confronting him in what must have been a humiliating trial all its own (Canetti, 1974). Kafka mounted a shabby defense, then retreated in defeat, as the engagement gradually dissolved.

In the *Letter to his Father* (1966), his comments on this affair form the heart of the matter, the humiliatingly botched engagement being 'the most grandiose and hopeful attempts at [my] escape ... their failure was correspondingly grandiose' (p. 89). Escape from what, we might wonder; from the fate of being Hermann's son perhaps, the scion of a tyrant equally clueless at life and love—as emulated by his hapless son.

Kafka connects this failed escape with his own 'weakness [and] lack of self-confidence, the sense of guilt [which] drew a cordon between myself and marriage' (p. 89). This after addressing his father's 'total lack of feeling for the suffering and shame you could inflict on me' (p. 17). Such ruinous shame became cumulative, as 'the older I became, the more material there was for you to bring up' (p. 33): a wretched yet intractable attachment. *In hating me you destroyed both of us,* Franz seems to say, both of them exiled, divided like the worm.

Kafka thus outlines his impossible position. By seeking marriage, Franz attempted to escape paternal imprisonment—yet in so doing he also repeated his father's exploitative character, by exploiting (or so he feared) Felice for said escape, a woman he loved and therefore obsessively distanced, ostensibly for *her* protection, due to the odiousness of his inherited character, in the distressing similarities between himself and Hermann.

This withdrawal, initially protective of his beloved, then becomes an abandonment of her: another appalling parallel with Hermann. Again, Franz sees himself as toxic due to his toxic psychic inheritance, his longings absurd or even irrelevant—never more so than in matters of romance, given the rottenness of the tree from which he fell.

I think this is the most anguishing source of Kafka's heartbreak. 'You and I are so alike, and I came from you,' he seems to say, 'how could you despise me?' By condemning his son, Hermann also condemned his son's love, so that Franz's yearning for recognition and foundational intimacy becomes verminous, sealing the fate of familial repetition. Franz both detested yet sought the source of darkness, that fateful attachment, trapped in foggy noxiousness, inescapably rotten yet dependent, a prisoner who escapes only to then faithfully rebuild his cell (an image borrowed from the *Letter*).

Kundera (1988) comments on Kafka's vividly grim fictional worlds of inscrutable organization wherein 'no one knows who programmed those laws ... they have nothing to do with human concerns and are thus unintelligible' (location 949). Such dehumanization leads the protagonist to feel that 'his entire existence is a mistake' (location 955). One cannot ever fulfill tyrannically imposed yet opaque ideals upon which the system is founded. This to me looms larger, contextually, than any details of antidotal escape, such as pornography or alcohol.

In the case of James in other words, why not browse soft porn on the internet? His own existence has already been found 'guilty.'

James also, at first, wrestled with prereflective guilt in pursuing his own differentiation with me—an abandonment of sorts of archaic relational ties. When he told me, '*she* doesn't see it that way,' he was in part stating the difficulty I was putting him in (vexing as it sounded to me), in risking fundamental differentiation (Brandchaft, 2010). Just crossing my threshold consistently was an achievement; my allowing that to be 'good enough' in discussing the affective function rather than the simple eradication of pornography helped our cause, as I understood how deeply he wanted to be seen as good rather than *only* burdensome, and how menacing was such a want to the systems of familiarity.

I also had to sit with the discomfort of seeing a grown man abused without any trace of self-assertion. But once I found a way to address the frightened boy he was never allowed to be, for whom Karen was scary, the more we both observed just how destructive was their repetitive dance, that the recognition he craved could not alas be found (as with me and my sponsor) because Karen too was an abandoned child, acting out as he 'acted in.'

One day in fact he mentioned he had finished a draft of his screenplay, which prompted my enthusiasm. I also recognized the difficulty of being 'found out' by Karen, who might lambast him for ignoring his domestic tasks. 'Thanks for understanding,' he said, 'I wish she did.' He then burst into tears, sobbing for several minutes. We had found the raw and aching heart of things, the boot momentarily lifted.

Then soon after, with *Kafkan* timing, his company announced they were relocating to the Northwest, offering James a financial offer he could not refuse, meaning he would see his family only on the weekends, and his analyst via Skype. He was dismayed how comfortable Karen was with this distance, in light of his juicy salary. We kept things going briefly long-distance, but his life was complicated, there were scores of chores afoot, and treatment gradually petered off.

I think of his treatment still, with hopefulness, similar to Kafka's description in his *Letter* of seeing his dad smile on very rare occasion, even waving to him playfully when he (Franz) was young. Franz held closely to that for life. My own father and I drove cross country together when I moved to Los Angeles from the East Coast, in 1996. This too was a kind of last hurrah. I got sober a few years later, which we discussed only once, nine or so years before he died.

***

Near the end of his life, Kafka fell in love with Dora Diamant, a devoted and loving partner. Kafka died in her arms, in a sanitarium, with the melancholy relief he likely felt upon reaching the end of a most anorexic existence, via an illness that was for him both curse and blessing (Pawel, 1991).

I think of James sobbing when we found that spot of tenderness, the painful pleasure of finding relational respite, a lifetime of loneliness expressed. This case illuminates for me the potential of relational mitigation, in light of childhood trauma never recognized, where vulnerability is 'guilty' of wanting a safety overburdening to *others*: a trial in which the person's own humanity is ever liable. When we observe such punishment as especially brutal for patients, we might easily squirm with a 'desperate feeling of powerlessness,' a tempting to rid ourselves of 'this unbearable feeling by offering the patient explanations that ignore his or her plight' (both Miller, 1998, p. 251).

Treatment remains arid until patients' plights become relationalized, deeply understood, with participants leaning into angst in the face of finitude and repetitive trauma, aided by an analyst asymmetrically vulnerable,. This accounts for the mostly useless suggestions I offered James, rather than explore his suffering alongside it rather than from afar. Finally doing so dispelled our parallel illusions of protection, both of us now together in the dock, guilty of fallibility, against the hanging judge of so many camouflaged tyrannies.

References

Atwood, G. (2015). Credo and reflections. *Psychoanalytic Dialogues*, 25(2): 137–152.

Atwood, G.E. & Stolorow, R.D. (2014). *Structures of subjectivity: Explorations in psychoanalytic phenomenology and contextualism* (2nd ed.). Routledge/Taylor & Francis Group.

Brandchaft, B. (2010). Systems of pathological accommodation in psychoanalysis. In B. Brandchaft, S. Doctors, & D. Sorter, *Toward an emancipatory psychoanalysis: Brandchaft's intersubjective vision* (pp. 193–220). New York: Routledge.

Canetti, E. (1974). *Kafka's other trial* (C. Middleton, trans.). New York, NY: Penguin Modern Classics.

Jones, B. (2009). Addiction and pathological accommodation: an intersubjective look at impediments to the utilization of Alcoholics Anonymous. *International Journal of Psychoanalytic Self Psychology*, 4(2): 212–234.

Jordison, S. (2017, May). Gabriel García Márquez: Working magic with 'brick-faced' realism. *The Guardian*. www.theguardian.com.

Kafka, F. (1946/2005). *The trial* (D. Wyllie, trans.) [ebook]. Project Gutenberg. www.gutenberg.org/ebooks/7849.

Kafka, F. (1948/1975). *Metamorphosis and other stories* (W. & E. Muir, trans.). New York, NY: Schocken Books.

Kafka, F. (1953/1966). *Letter to his father* (E. Kaiser & E. Wilkins, trans.) New York, NY: Schocken Books.

Kafka, F. (1967/1973). *Letters to Felice* (E. Duckworth & J. Stern, trans.). New York, NY: Schocken Books.

Khantzian, E.J. (1995). Self-regulation vulnerabilities in substance abusers: Treatment implications. In S. Cowling, *The Psychology and Treatment of Addictive Behavior* (pp. 17–41). Madison, CT: International Universities Press.

Kohut, H. (1975). The future of psychoanalysis. *The Annual of Psychoanalysis*, 3: 325–340.

Kundera, M. (1988). *The art of the novel* (L. Asher, trans.) [ebook]. New York, NY: Grove Press.

Miller, A. (1981/1998). *Thou shalt not be aware: Society's betrayal of the child* (H. & H. Hannum, trans.). New York, NY: Farrar, Straus & Giroux.

Ogden, T. (2009). Kafka, Borges, and the creation of consciousness, Part I: Kafka—Dark ironies of the 'gift' of consciousness. *Psychoanalytic Quarterly*, 78(2): 343–367.

Pawel, E. (1984/1991). *The nightmare of reason*. New York, NY: Farrar, Straus & Giroux.

Schafer, R. (1997). Vicissitudes of remembering in the countertransference: Fervent failure, colonisation and remembering otherwise. *International Journal of Psychoanalysis*, 78: 1151–1163.

Socarides, D. & Stolorow, R.D. (1984). Affects and selfobjects. *Annual of Psychoanalysis*, 12: 105–119.

Stolorow, R.D. (2015). A phenomenological-contextual, existential, and ethical perspective on emotional trauma. *Psychoanalytic Review*, 102(1): 123–138.

Stolorow, R.D. & Atwood, G.E. (1992). *Contexts of being: The intersubjective foundations of psychological life*. Hillsdale, NJ: Analytic Press, Inc.

Stolorow, R.D. & Atwood, G.E. (2016). Walking the tightrope of emotional dwelling. *Psychoanalytic Dialogues*, 26(1): 103–108.

Winnicott, D.W. (1971). *Playing and reality*. Oxon, UK: Routledge.

Chapter 7

Simulated Selfhood, Authentic Dialogue

An Intersubjective-Systems Look at Treating Addiction

'Stop Overanalyzing': Treatment Begins

The outcome of this case reminds me of this notion from Martin Buber (1970) about the I-You or intersubjective encounter:

> What counts is not these products of analysis and reflection but the genuine original unity, the lived relationship.
>
> (p. 70)

Not that it started that way. New patient Tyler told me he was 'facing forty,' living in a converted garage next to his mother's house; he also stated his mother, Betty, was a 'nag and pain in the ass.' He had acquiesced to her demand to see me so she would 'back off.'

Tyler said he smoked 'a joint or two' most days, 'but so does half of L.A.' He drank and took a Xanax 'occasionally,' sometimes watched porn, sought paid companionship 'once in a blue moon,' adding emphatically that 'I'm *not* a goddamn addict,' as Betty insisted.

He then related melancholy but warm memories of his father, who had died eight years earlier in a car accident; a successful, 'workaholic' television producer, he was exhausted one evening and fell asleep at the wheel. Tyler blamed his mother for this as well, as 'she literally nagged him to death.' (I also suspected early on that his home almost literally symbolized his father, leading to a preserved attachment, albeit concretized.)

Tyler was not exactly eager to begin; I sensed he would rather be digging a ditch. 'I don't see the point of therapy, no offense,' he remarked, 'I'm only here to keep her off my back. So I smoke a little weed. Who wouldn't, living with a psycho.' Tyler was blunt, and quite intelligent ... arousing my curiosity about his apparent lack of any ambition or direction.

Meanwhile I noticed my own unease, even pangs of dread, arising early in treatment. Was it that Tyler was there so reluctantly, leaving me a kind of passive babysitter?

DOI: 10.4324/9781003266358-8

All of his problems stemmed from his mother, was his conviction, including the estrangement of a beloved half-sister, from his father's first marriage; she was 'way cool,' but aloof, thanks to Betty. Some of this reminded me of some my own original family's alcoholic divisiveness and chaos, which added to the discomfort.

Tyler and his mother bickered frequently, with a volatile, tragicomic edge. As is often the case with systems marked by chaotic, intensely fraught enmeshments (Brandchaft, 2002), or mutually enslaving relational ties, it often felt as though Betty were *in the room with us*, so ruminatively apprehensive and angry was he over her embittered perception of him as a 'loser.' At the same time, such rumination also seemed like a deflection from something significant yet elusive, or stubbornly unformulated (Stern, 2003).

His lack of interest in any therapeutic direction also chafed. But then he seemed removed from relational engagement in general; his one 'friend' was his pot dealer. He had no romantic interests, apparently content with pornography alone. This also irritated Mom, who for the most part supported him (and his treatment), though he did hold a part time job, at a pot dispensary.

For Tyler, a cigar was *always* only a cigar. Thus, our inability to discuss occasional clinical turbulence: he sometimes arrived or cancelled late, agitated if I 'read into it,' as for instance possible ambivalence. Finally, I had to say that for us to continue, he would have to arrive more or less on time for our weekly meeting.

He shrugged indifferently and said, 'Fine.'

Meanwhile Betty began calling for updates: 'Does he know he's an addict? I'll bet he's a sex addict too! Does he need rehab?' I was reluctant to talk to her, but Tyler practically begged me, as it (again) kept her away from him. Thus I emailed brief, generic overviews.

There were occasional remarks from him like, 'you're a decent dude' or 'thanks for listening,' soon obscured by bitter ranting about having to be there, or other matters arousing his ire. Finally, I asked if there were *anything* he wanted help with.

'Nope,' he said, going on another rant about the banalities of Hollywood. Still I intuited he enjoyed having someone there to listen, rather than simply scold. Perhaps it also helped him feel in control, as I felt a bit handcuffed.

I expressed a keen interest in his passion for film editing. 'It's all too commercialized,' he sighed, as *any* sustained inquiry went nowhere, even as I feared 'leaning back' might echo his father's abandonment. None of this was available for discussion. Nor was his anger, flaring when I tried to 'overanalyze' his rage towards mom, whose tyranny was 'obvious,' in his view.

His mother's calls became more frequent, with arguments at home more intense.

'I hope there's progress,' she would say, 'His anger scares me ... I might need to call the cops!' Perhaps they would intervene, I momentarily, darkly fancied ... and take the case off my hands.

Under the Rock: Working with Addiction

Working with addiction can be Sisyphean, in cases where our desire to help patients becomes an 'unspeakable penalty in ... accomplishing nothing' (Camus, 1983, p. 120). Camus, in his essay *The Myth of Sisyphus*, uses 'absurdity' to describe such futility, a term I have indicated as useful in describing dyadic frustration, or clinically fraught experiences (see Chapter 3).

'Absurdity' is an apt term to describe treating addiction. It often appears early, with patients and analysts prone to alienation from each other's or even *their own* subjectivity, a process which the analyst holds as exploratory or reflective as the patient awaits a provision of 'cures.' Analysts look to nurture the understanding of emotional experience, running into barriers when approaching developmental strivings deemed *inarguably* toxic in patients' self-organizations. The strivings we might want to nurture, or understand, are dangerous to patients' self-ideals of strength (without drugs or alcohol, one of these days), within noxious relational contexts reinforcing such ideals, saturated by binary personality organizations that idealize strength and pathologize fallibility or 'weakness.'

Such a harrowing or psychically agitating binary, between yearnings that conflict with contextual demands for disavowal (the self-ideal), is fertile breeding ground for addiction, which soothes the gap. It provides at least a simulacrum of fleeting authenticity, a virtual selfhood. Alcohol, for instance, may mitigate social anxiety, helping the drinker be more 'themselves.' Cocaine can provide a fleeting sense of euphoric self-empowerment or expansiveness (the latter holds true for pot as well), momentarily but potently offsetting self-doubt, repressive uncertainty, or other addictive vulnerabilities (Khantzian, 2003).

Meanwhile, the transferential pull on analysts, to provide reliable bypassing of such potentially destabilizing affect, might echo analysts' own archaic family experience, wherein children's vulnerability required denunciation in favor of attunement to *caregivers*. This is the 'gifted child' phenomenon (Miller, 1979), or what Atwood (2015) calls the 'little psychotherapist' scenario. In such scenarios, children are required to 'sustain a depressed or otherwise emotionally troubled parent ... the child is not allowed to become the person he or she might have been' (p. 150). Such imprisonment reflects the distressing absurdity of a radioactivity to a child's developmental essence; years later, an analyst encounters a patient's hyper-reactive context in which hints of authenticity are threatening; in other words, these patients often hope analysts will also conform to contextual demands. This can mean the *analyst* perceives she cannot become the caregiver-figure she hopes to be, leading possibly to dyadic stuckness, or impasse.

The powerfully repetitive, centrifugal force of compulsive aversions in such systems can leave analysts feeling stymied or deflated. The entrenchment of such contextually enforced protections have even, for this analyst, seemed to make a mockery of an enterprise which favors reflectivity or introspection. This rigid 'emotional tyranny' can echo my own archaic experiencing of accommodating addicted parents. Thus, Tyler's worldhood, where marijuana and porn served as efficient antidotes for the pain of amputated selfhood, became for me a dark attractor state (Stolorow, 1997), leading to oddly powerful impulses to somehow *ensure* his emotional safety, the both of us dancing around unthinkable trauma-affect.

Archaically, in such contexts, a child or 'little psychoanalyst' may come to feel her own authentic needs are 'harmful' to addicted or compromised caregivers. Analogously, the adult analyst may anxiously apprehend her own analytic hopes as 'too much' for patients struggling with their own (or loved ones') addiction.

How to untangle all this, with patients eager for antidotal foreclosure, where we might begin to feel like a bottle or pill in human form?

One of the notions I have found helpful is noticing how compulsively maintained diversions, including attachments to addictive substances or processes, parallel patients' contextual 'ideology' disfavoring vulnerability. Such contexts are often characterized by rapidly oscillating feeling-states, and rigidity or chaos, with epistemological contradictions that can leave the listener bewildered (e.g., 'I am probably going to kill myself, but don't worry I'll never do it, though things are hopeless, also I just met someone cool on this dating app'). Even some sober patients, in recovery programs, subsist within a context demanding accommodation (Jones, 2009) rather than a *relational* way of easing or even recognizing distress. Addicted patients, generally speaking, are new to the concept of relational process. Many have never been permitted to *think about,* let alone articulate, traumatic feeling-states to an empathic other; such states thus become a reflexive call to detour. Even when we believe we are expressing only *mild* empathic curiosity, this curiosity can provoke a fear or terror of breakdown (Winnicott, 1974).

Such states are often the result of biphasic developmental trauma, experiences of 1) the profound neglect, abuse, or abandonment of the child, pain which is then 2) minimized, invalidated, or deemed toxic *to the caregiver,* thus the child's core sense of safety (Stolorow, 2015).

In this case, it was (primarily) the chaotic intensity of Tyler's self-protections *and* the intensity of his dedifferentiating context, often behaviorally enacted, that startled or provoked my own halting uncertainty—or determined burst of curiosity, which Tyler often perceived as intrusive. Meanwhile his ambivalence was, at times, itself a diversion from the contextually 'controversial' use of pot or porn, *itself* a diversion from the (unacknowledged) abandonment-pain of his father's absence, and mother's annihilations, together with contextually unseen intergenerational trauma. It took us a long time to tap into the fear and shame rooted in Tyler's centralizing and agonizing sense of unworthiness and neglect. Betty's ongoing attacks only reinforced his self-protections, reified his perceptions of her apparent contempt of him, *especially his needing marijuana,* to deal with searing emptiness and isolation.

It took time for me to see that Tyler had no good reason to trust me; for starters, he did not know me. It is easy to overlook this, and the risk patients take just by stepping into my office. How can they know I will not become another abandoning or annihilating figure, which transferentially is *likely* to occur, given my own inevitable fallibility (Orange, 1995)? Absurdly enough, it is sometimes the intensity of my own keen hopes of being 'good enough,' even a subtle seeking of recognition of my benevolent intentions, that can be perceived as demanding; patient 'blowback' is sometimes followed by my withdrawal, initially to 'give them space' while serving as a self-protection of my own. Reflecting upon all this became the *decisive* (Brandchaft, 2010) issue in slowly developing dialogue with Tyler, making space for understanding his own distinctively unique perception and experiencing, while clearing my own analytic 'fog.'

The case in other words asked of *me* a heightened and more vulnerable self-reflection, in parallel to the analytic 'ask' of the patient. In clearing the way to a distinctive recognition of Tyler's dilemma; in seeing *him* and his tightly camouflaged strivings, in a way Betty could not, I made it safer for him to recognize *me,* and the potentiality of our relatedness. At first, the intensity of his aversions became (for me) a determination to thwart our process, since mother (like my own caregivers) 'demanded it,' and he complied, the two of them *together* becoming deflating family-figures, repetitively demanding my compliance.

In fact, Brandchaftian (2010) accommodation is often a theme in such cases; the drug or drink 'accommodates' the patient in soothing the pain of the compulsion to accommodate a dysphoric system. But addiction can enslave even the treatment, leading to patients' concretization of experience, or antidotal demands. This in turn can provoke a possibly mutual disillusionment, resentment, even a hidden shame, in 'failing' (transferentially) the other's expectations or hopes.

It is helpful to keep an eye on how an enmeshed relationship *with the drug or drink itself* parallels the emotional aversiveness of the person's relational context, especially with patients struggling with compliance, rage, and other self-protections. Addictive activity becomes a centralizing metaphor of a world prohibiting vulnerable strivings, demanding ideals of self-reliance that then necessitate relief. The cycle of protection and abuse, safety and imprisonment (Brandchaft, 2010), found in noxious caregiver systems, becomes manifest in addictive cycling also; euphoria gives way to hangover, confidence to shame or self-criticism, followed again by a need for relief. *Addiction imprisons as it protects, abuses as it soothes.*

Compulsive behaviors initially enlivening or restorative (Stolorow & Atwood, 2014) eventually enslave, as more of the substance is needed to 'do the job.' Yet absurdly, such antidotal provision is often more effective initially than actual caregivers! Such 'virtual' emancipation also eases the terror (and craving) of fundamental differentiation (Brandchaft, 2010), within systemic enmeshments.

This is but one reason patients living with addiction, or addicted others, are intensely ambivalent about taking up with a new caregiver figure who will likely (and however benevolently), sooner or later, suggest that they 'sober up' and/or 'start focusing on your own well-being,' as the latter eludes perception entirely. This is especially true with 'doghouse' therapy, common in my practice, where patients land in trouble with loved ones (the doghouse), for drinking or drugging, forced into therapy/penance for an arbitrary period. Some stay, most do not. Those who leave sometimes overdose, or commit suicide. This is but one reason I try to persevere, at least keep open an invitation to proceed.

Still, nascent analytic rapport is complexified by a bristling ambivalence common to those who have found *their own* reliably provisional 'companion,' an addictive attachment style pulsing with contradiction. Most addicted patients have never had good reason to trust any symbolic or actual caregivers, as any primal vulnerability remains camouflaged by an 'allergic' self-protection, a wariness of 'reading into' one's own affective experience, lest it again be destroyed or deemed insignificant.

With all this in mind, it becomes clear that analysts are initially facing, even 'taking on' *an entire intersubjective context.* So present are the crucial others in the patient's life that it can even become perplexing as to whose subjectivity we are addressing in our offices.

This is likely why Brandchaft underscored the decisiveness of analysts' own ongoing self-reflection—combined with a continuing empathic investigation (Stolorow, 1993) of our impact on patients. This highlights, to my mind, the benefit of an intersubjective-systems approach, as sustained curiosity about patients' meaning-making (Stolorow, 2015) of analysts, however primitive, while keeping an eye on our own analytic meaning-making, are potential pathways to loosening constriction and clinical creativity (Orange, 2010). Patients may be reluctant to respond and quick to enact, yet curiosity about their experience of us can eventually disconfirm archaic indifference, even when such possibility provokes repetitive anxiety (itself worth investigating).

This can co-exist with behavioral options, such as outside support between sessions (such as AA). A willingness to step outside the bounds of the 'usual,' as best we can—as a therapist once steered me into AA with fatherly firmness—can be meaningful for patients; it disconfirms the *cordon sanitaire,* with a willingness for us to 'be real' or 'get our hands dirty,' unlike distracted caregivers or former therapists. My interest in the emotional provisions of addiction, for example, can reflects a novel desire to know *them* rather than an induction for them to 'clean up your act.'

There is no formula. How could there be, given the complexity of human subjectivity, to say nothing of intersubjectivity, or the interhuman (Buber,

1999)—combined with the labyrinthine nature of addictive processes? Such chaos, rigidity, and affective intensity can test the limits of our resourcefulness or patience. But our ongoing curiosity about the possible meanings of patients' experience *of us*, and therapeutic process, even when they struggle to articulate them (though they often have a way of letting us know) can gradually mitigate patients' archaic terrors.

Addicted patients tend to cherish occasionally raw spontaneity, or 'keeping it real.' There is room for trial and error. It is helpful to be cognizant of recovery programs; still, there is no replacement for a persistent curiosity about a patient's own experience and perspective. (A person's longings and terrors influence any relational field, recognized or not.) Keeping dialogic possibility alive, as best we can, just might save the patient's life.

'Virtual Selfhood' is Better than None

Given the incommensurability of our respective stances, some 'head-butting' was inevitable. Despite fleeting moments of melancholy and woundedness, Tyler remained wedded to compulsive affective detouring, the rigidity of which became antagonistic to the way I worked. (Too much absurdity gives one a headache.)

Thus, Tyler one day asked if I would email his mother and demand she stop rummaging through his room and browsing history. He tried a lock on his door; she broke it, since 'it's *my* property, dad left it to *me*.' (I wanted to send them both to their room.)

I understood such enraging intrusiveness; what rankled was that his 'ask' sounded like a demand. (Much as his mother related to him, I imagined.)

He said, annoyed at my hesitation, 'This would help me, and that's your job isn't it?'

My empathically reflecting the rank injustice of being 'monitored' only underscored that I 'should' do this. He said I was again 'overthinking it.' We went back and forth a few times, tension rising, when I suddenly paused and said, 'You really miss your dad, don't you.'

He hesitated a few moments. Silence. Then he nodded, eyes watering.

Just before uttering that phrase I was thinking, *I won't do this, he can't make me!* I found myself in a kind of rabbit hole, or mini-flashback, wherein I was again, as the oldest and 'most responsible' of three siblings, *forced* by my parents to parent others, including them, painfully squelching my own agency and spontaneity, no one looking out for the overburdened child.

These associations gelled like lightning, along with some of Tyler's sad recollections of his father; suddenly the patient seemed to be tugging at my sleeve, like an earnest, anxious little boy.

In following sessions, he related times when his dad did intervene with mom, which was all the more reason why he missed him now. I sensed there were not many such interventions; despite Tyler's affection and idealization of his father, the latter (I intuited) preferred to be at work, rather than home with his wife. Thus, young Tyler was caught in the tug of war, a neglected casualty.

Yet Tyler, starting from a young age, often worried about *his mother's* emotional state, in accepting the 'man of the house' role implicitly handed to him. Here again, a caregiver's feeling-states became centralizing, in this case including rage, neglect, and the implication of his fragile yearnings being 'too much' for his protectors. The seeds of an inflexible self-ideal, and need for addictive relief, were planted in profusion; he had to stay close to an invalidating caregiver.

Tyler and I reached a compromise. He would draft an email to mom, *with my help*. He did so in a firm but surprisingly gentle way.

'I would feel less stress if you would please stay out,' he told her. She agreed, to our pleasant surprise, and he thanked me in a warm email.

This in turn gave me confidence that there was in fact more going on than met the eye, that I was not 'deluding myself' in thinking he had begun to trust me; perhaps we had become (asymmetrical) siblings in gifted childhood (Miller, 1979). This also, I should add, encouraged me to set my own boundary with *her*, which Tyler finally understood, sensing I too felt intruded upon. Tendrils of developmental transference took hold: a brotherly twin-ship, together with my fatherly recognition and validation of his maternally repetitive retraumatizations.

This led to another epiphany. During one of his rants about Betty's ongoing attacks, I again felt handcuffed: the tug of my own child-self drew me back, to boyhood moments where I was taken hostage, forced to listen and echo aloud my father's slurry monologues—to adopt *his* perspective, to reflect the worthiness he needed to see, lest I receive scalding criticism. I sensed Tyler likely felt this with his mother, in a way never acknowledged by anyone.

I interrupted him and said, 'I think I see why you *have* to smoke pot.' He paused, intrigued, as I speculated that the frustrating disappointments of an absurdly indifferent world were offset by the 'homey' world of pornography and pot, a safety his actual home-world, or *his own mother*, could not provide. (Here I again drew on my own emotional analogues and experience, including my own recovery process and reflections gleaned therein.)

'Right!' he said, an electricity in the room.

I began to understand how he—in addition to his wondering whether I was truly on *his* side—had long felt forced to soothe *his mother*, such bene-volence unrecognized in the vaporous heat of her wrath. Her emotional assaults combined noxiously with her (absurd) insistence that he give up the very thing he found effective in tolerating her repetitive maternal failures.

I wondered aloud if his rage at her was not so much because smoke or drink was harmful, as she insisted (which he in fact agreed with!), but because she refused to recognize a need for relief *she herself had never provided*.

'Man,' I said, 'that's nuts! I'd smoke pot too!'

'Right!' he said again. 'It's like she's punishing me for my dealing with her craziness.' Then, quietly: 'And for loving dad more than her. She was always jealous of that.' Again, his eyes welled up, and I felt that strange reassurance when sorrow or grief makes its way into a patient's heretofore restricted range of expression.

From there we eased into a bumpy yet expansive phase, not without more tumult and limit-setting, though Tyler surprised me by agreeing to meet three times a week. He also surprised me by enrolling in classes, to finish his film degree, and attempting online dating. Also unprompted was a stated desire to ease his 'vices,' as he wanted to be more alert for class, and 'chicks really hate porn, understandably.' He said, with a hint of shame, that he 'might be a little addicted' to pornography, adding, 'please don't tell mom.' We discussed a course of harm reduction (Tatarsky, 2002), determining small steps to reduce use. (Harm reduction is often more 'user friendly' than total abstinence.) Finally, he told me he was thinking of finding his own place.

Yet it was much harder to move out than either of us anticipated, in surrendering the last fluctuating wisps of hope of winning Betty's approval. It is easy to underestimate such camouflaged desires in the 'heat of battle,' provoking a question as to who is protecting whom in such contexts.

This was even more confounding since mom expressed not pride in his taking these forward steps, but criticism for his not starting sooner, wasting 'years of your life,' for seeking an 'impractical film degree,' all of this stated of course 'for your own good.' He avoided arguing, while baffled and a bit ashamed of his hesitance to leave. This is often the case (with accommodation, for instance) when a person's self-esteem takes a beating for not having the strength to 'shrug off' existential imprisonment. It also demoralized him to encounter difficulty in stopping pornography, as pot was set aside rather easily. Again, harm reduction proved useful. (Sexual compulsivity can be astonishingly difficult to reduce or halt.)

We had far to go, but I was proud of him for not giving up. He struggled to have faith in himself, but developed a faith, of his own volition, that *my* faith in him, at least, might be genuine.

Straddling the Canyon: Concluding Thoughts

Buber (1999) describes the abyss or void encountered by the therapist in understanding a patient: an existential darkness or fraught uncertainty, often constituted by both parties' apprehension that the relationship may not survive—an anxiety possibly leading to mutually constrictive self-protections. Addictive processes only intensify such protections, and the aversion to reflecting on all of the above; in these cases, treatment often *begins* at disjunction or impasse.

Meanwhile the effort or debilitation resulting from such compulsive aversion—the costs of maintaining one's 'self-medicating' activity—continue to be organized as sources of paralyzing self-loathing, as traumatic affect itself remains locked away. Paralyzing shame is also often deflected, in line with rigid self-ideals—a pressure which, again, leads to a craving for relief.

Addicted patients, as embedded within their respective relational systems, are often passionately, stubbornly resistant to change, while valuing an individualism that may sound absurdly Sisyphean to a relational-minded analyst, yet essential to a patient hoping for the warmth of intimacy while remaining 'armored.' Alcohol or drugs might solve this contradiction, temporarily, in providing soothing, or a fleeting albeit hopeful emancipation that allows patients to rest within or hold onto *their own mind or point of view*; hallucinogens such as pot or LSD might even, as with Tyler, stimulate untapped aspects of a person's systemically discouraged creative or relational aspirations.

The devil of it is that addictive processes, including their numbing of vulnerability, are initially the perfect antidotes for existential despair or loneliness, as they are chosen and 'controlled' by the person alone, like a transitional object, while further obscuring whatever fuels or underlies such a pervasively isolated-mind perspective. Such *family* organizing is slow to loosen, as antidotal means of tolerating such chaotic, volatile, and searingly painful emotional environs have already been *a way of life*, the *lingua franca* of addictive-family relating. In this way we are often, at the outset, asking patients to reorient themselves entirely, possibly provoking an analysts' historical apprehension of asking 'too much' from others, even as we witness systemic suffering. (One toxic legacy of relational trauma is the reactive bond between longing and danger.)

At the same time, hard-won clinical experience leaves me optimistic that a relational analysis, even when combined with adjunct support such as recovery meetings, can be powerfully transformative over time, in our seeking to understand (rather than reactively seek to mitigate) the relational roots of addictive processes and what pain *they* seek to mitigate. Our own subjective responses to such contexts are also useful, with patients' terror of vulnerability serving at times as a window into my own archaic allergy to fallibility, the temptation of 'safe' antidotal detouring. Such hesitation can then provoke patients' fears of overwhelming the other, an aversiveness cyclically expanding.

This is why patients struggling with addiction, on a spectrum from mild to acute, are often also, over time, appreciative of my well-timed transparency of frankly-stated intent or aim, as well as my recognizing my own fallibility or misattunements, relieving them in some cases of a sense of overburdening. What is dyadically grounding is simply a sustained curiosity about their distinctiveness or genuine 'take' on things, even the provocation of longstanding terrors, such as transferential fears of disappointing me during enactments, or via their repeated self-protections, gradually revealed as adaptive necessity. Thus our sustained curiosity, often combined with humor and spontaneity, becomes an ally in the protection of analytic space, and the patient's expansiveness—a protection both benevolent or intrusive, and open for discussion.

I am often surprised by my own yearning for certainty amidst addictive whirlwind. With addiction, after all, analysts can feel they are facing a hurricane, or straddling an abyss between the patient's anxious wish for 'riddance,' and an analytical developmental hope for expansive relatedness. Meanwhile, patients' seeking antidotes or the riddance of vulnerability dovetail with my own archaic demands for antidotal hyperattunement, as if I am again expected to perfectly adapt or even *be* the other person. (Many patients, terrified of vulnerability and new to relational process, hope for exactly this.) It can be bewildering at first as to who is tying whose hands; chaos, rigidity, and lurking enmeshment seems to characterize so many early treatments.

In the early days of seeing Tyler, I perceived a demand to fit myself to the needs of his family, and resented it. I simultaneously wondered if this case 'ought' to be so difficult, that I was possibly failing my own beloved theorists and mentors. Thus it became necessary to disentangle some of my *own* repetitive transferences, in clearing perspectival space for the patient's.

The void of uncertainty that might provoke a patient's fear of breakdown (Winnicott, 1974) is also constituted by the vastness of new possibility; bounded by finitude, yet unbounded by the unknown, untapped relational potential, as both weary aspiration and terror fill the void.

Addiction however seems to almost cynically assert *precisely* where we are headed, in averting both risk and potential vulnerability, lending antidotal certainly while sneakily derailing developmental potential. Such disabling is itself numbed or deflected, a cycle now tolerable *or preferred* in its anesthetizing familiarity. The 'Godot' (Beckett, 1954) I myself await is thus often, for the patient, a terrifying unknown.

The work *is* indeed risky (Buber, 1999), as some addicted patients initially apprehend even the slightest misattunement as betrayal, stemming from an archaic context where fallibility is contemptible. Some prefer a 'speedier' route such as EMDR, CBT, or other acronymic solutions.

The noble attempt to redeem our own historically disavowed trauma, as psychoanalysts is both developmental and repetitive for dyadic process; expansive mutuality also provokes asymmetrical (Aron, 1996) retraumatization. This of course includes analysts from addictive backgrounds, hoping to apply such agonizing early experience to useful ends. It may even be our *own* difficult or painful personal analyses that best serve our patients, as we stumble upon segregated self-experience that we are not initially keen to revisit. Still, relational analysis provides opportunity to mitigate the imprisonment of addictive processes wrought, in most cases, by relational trauma itself. Given the prevalence of addiction societally, and the position we are in to understand such patients at depth, I believe the risk is well worth taking.

References

Agassi, J.B. (Ed.). (1999). *Martin Buber on psychology and psychotherapy.* Syracuse University Press.

Aron, L. (1996). *A meeting of minds.* London & Hillsdale, NJ: The Analytic Press.

Atwood, G.E. (2015). Credo and reflections. *Psychoanalytic Dialogues,* 25: 137–152.

Atwood, G.E. & Stolorow, R.D. (2014). *Structures of subjectivity: Explorations in psychoanalytic phenomenology and contextualism* (2nd ed.). Oxon, UK: Routledge.

Beckett, S. (1954). *Waiting for Godot.* New York: Grove Press.

Brandchaft, B. (2002). Reflections on the intersubjective foundations of the sense of self: Commentary on paper by Steven Stern. *Psychoanalytic Dialogues,* 12(5): 727–745.

Brandchaft, B. (2010). Systems of pathological accommodation in psychoanalysis. In B. Brandchaft, S. Doctors, & D. Sorter, *Toward an emancipatory psychoanalysis: Brandchaft's intersubjective vision* (pp. 193–220). New York: Routledge.

Buber, M. (1970). *I and Thou* (W.A. Kaufmann, trans.). New York: Scribner.

Buber, M. (1999). Elements of the interhuman. In J.B. Agassi (Ed.), *Martin Buber on psychology and psychotherapy: Essays, letters, and dialogue.* Syracuse, NY: Syracuse University Press.

Camus, A. (1983). *The myth of Sisyphus* (J. O'Brien, trans.). New York: Alfred A. Knopf.

Coburn, W. (2017). Commensurability and incommensurability of paradigms among theories and persons. *Psychoanalysis, Self and Context,* 12(2): 163–172.

Jones, D.B. (2009). Addiction and pathological accommodation: An intersubjective look at impediments to the utilization of Alcoholics Anonymous. *International Journal of Psychoanalytic Self Psychology,* 4: 212–234.

Khantzian, E.J. (2003). Understanding addictive vulnerability: An evolving psychodynamic perspective. *Neuropsychoanalysis,* 5(1): 5–21.

Miller, A. (1979). The drama of the gifted child and the psychoanalyst's narcissistic disturbance. *International Journal of Psychoanalysis,* 60: 47–58.

Orange, D.M. (1995). *Emotional understanding.* New York: Guilford Press.

Orange, D.M. (2010). *Thinking for clinicians: Philosophical resources for contemporary psychoanalysis and the humanistic psychotherapies.* New York: Routledge.

Stern, D.B. (2003). *Unformulated experience: From dissociation to imagination.* New York: Routledge.

Stolorow, R.D. (1993). Thoughts on the nature and therapeutic action of psychoanalytic interpretation. *Progress in Self Psychology,* 9: 31–43.

Stolorow, R.D. (1997). Dynamic, dyadic, intersubjective systems: An evolving paradigm for psychoanalysis. *Psychoanalytic Psychology,* 14: 337–346.

Stolorow, R.D. (2007). *Trauma and human existence.* New York: Analytic Press.

Stolorow, R.D. (2015). Meaning is where the action is [blog post]. Retrieved from www.psychologytoday.com/us/blog/feeling-relating-existing/201503/meaning-is-where-the-action-is.

Stolorow, R.D. & Atwood, G. (2016). Walking the tightrope of emotional dwelling. *Psychoanalytic Dialogues,* 26(1): 103–108.

Tatarsky, A. (Ed.) (2002). *Harm reduction psychotherapy.* Lanham, MD: Jason Aronson.

Winnicott, D.W. (1974). Fear of breakdown. *International Review of Psycho-Analysis,* 1: 103–107.

Chapter 8

Reflections in the Fog

Transferential Challenges and COVID-19

Introduction

In this chapter, I explore the existential impact of pandemic life, leading to heightened clinical anxieties amidst challenges of maintaining connections—in some cases losing the relationship altogether due to viral contingencies.

Albert Camus, in his essay *The Myth of Sisyphus* (1942), introduces the term absurdity to describe such unexpected contingencies and our own finitude. Camus primarily focused on the unthinkability of death; in this discussion I focus upon relational or symbolic deaths, including the loss of face-to-face meetings, now marred by distance, technical glitches, and stalled connections. Some patients even stopped treatment, including those suddenly unemployed. The challenge of managing my own angst compounded unexpected challenges, including clinically. Yet such challenges also illuminated emotional analogues with patients, as illustrated in the case vignette below.

With Jan, the mother of an addicted son, I discover that my own subjective overwhelm becomes a window into the alienation and overwhelm that she too repetitively faces—only this time, her traumatic archaic experience is validated and recognized with new clarity through the COVID-related fog. We find each other via a hard-won alliance: siblings in viral uncertainty. This resonates with Camus' insistence that we not bow down to the contingencies of absurdity, no matter how formidable.

Uncertainty and Finitude, ad nauseum

Though some observers have drawn parallels between our current pandemic and Camus' novel *The Plague* (1948), I have of late found even greater resonance with his earlier essay, *The Myth of Sisyphus* (1942). This is not to diminish the novel, though Camus himself was never satisfied with it (Lottman, 1997); there remain intriguing parallels between the novel's ironic observations and the jarring finitude of the moment, again revealing our mortal vulnerability as an underlying human condition (de Botton, 2020).

DOI: 10.4324/9781003266358-9

In Chapter 3, I illustrated parallels between Camus and an array of psychoanalytic absurdities, specifically participants' experience of futility, the apparent maligning of analytic hopes. Camus describes absurdity as linked to our cosmic vulnerability, possibly undermining or threatening our resolve. I often observe it as any variety of analytic disappointments or retraumatizations, including threats to the relationship itself.

Sisyphus' punishment of eternal futility resembles for Camus our eventual answering to the gods, our human finitude: the heart of vulnerability. Sisyphus' crime was cheating Hades in the hope of gaining just a little more life, which angered the gods. Camus wonders what it is that keeps us going, when existential futility presses upon us while we crave a little more life, or living, the only certainty being finitude's arrival. Analogously I wonder what sustains analysis, as participants seek an asymmetrical transcendence or redemption, rather than a dreaded return to isolating torment—also inevitable, despite our strenuous efforts.

In my own case, such repetition includes a fear of inadequacy, of failing the patient in some way, tracing back to archaic compulsions to 'perfectly' accommodate caregivers. Historically for me, growing up in the rigid chaos of an addictive family, to 'fail' was to risk scalding criticism, a developmental death of its own.

Yet disappointing patients, leading possibly to their disillusionment, withdrawal, or rage is also inevitable or even necessary, when for instance patients cradle illusions of antidotal cure. Patients struggling with addiction often arrive in hope of a relief as quick as a drink or pill, or a 'toolkit' to permanently avert a lifetime of unrecognized pain, an escape analogous to Sisyphus' fugitive attempts. Patients' anxiety in such situations (especially during a crisis) can become dyadically contagious, as I find myself increasingly on edge.

Sooner or later most patients realize, not always happily, that the road to transformation runs through and not around such dreaded feeling-states. Even those patients asking me to 'hold their feet to the fire,' commandeer with tough-love, are often seeking to detour archaically-held shame, in enacting rather than exploring archaic affectivity—the pain of accommodating others for instance, a deeply familiar (often prereflective) dynamic in which they now ask me to participate. Meanwhile any sustained vulnerability—perhaps a dormant striving to be validated, seen—remains 'locked down,' reflexively quarantined, as inflexible dynamics are preserved.

Sooner or later, and despite anxieties to the contrary, patients' vulnerabilities emerge, self-protections slip—sometimes after experiencing a misattunement on the part of the analyst. Many patients initially imagine themselves to be far more transparent and readily 'knowable' than I experience them. They may be disappointed or confused that they have to 'explain' themselves. Or I might misread the moment or err on the side of caution for fear of re-injuring the patient, 'hanging back' for longer than necessary, provoking patients' anxieties of being seen as difficult or troubled, in need of kid gloves. Indeed, my own repetitive transference gets activated, as I dread when patients may respond like irritable caregivers, unhappy at my inadequate attunement to them, garnering what is to me a repetitive response such as, 'why are you killing me?' (Atwood, 2015, p. 150).

Asymmetrical, dyadic disappointment is in other words inevitable; my own Sisyphean attempt to escape from an archaic Hades is thwarted, a hope of helping the patient smoothly and without distress: one of my frequent analytic illusions, which when over-enforced ties my own hands, leading to analytic lockdown. This is also how it felt as COVID flourished, our leaders distracted, illusions dashed, isolation now inevitable.

***

I felt haunted by a hard-to-pinpoint sense of loss when the quarantine took hold, as I said goodbye to face to face meetings with patients, a handful of whom—to my surprise—said they would rather not meet via telephone or Zoom. I almost wondered if I were making a mistake in not continuing in person, despite the warnings of public health officials. (One young adult patient remarked, in regard to stopping altogether, 'I'll be sitting out the virus for now.') Some lost their job and could no longer afford treatment; some accepted my offer of sliding scale, while others insisted on waiting until they could pay.

Suddenly I appreciated the office itself, after many years of building a practice, developing a safe protected space now lost. A few patients conveyed shock at such disappearance, the cutoff of an environment dedicated to the recognition of their own distinctive (and to me sacred) subjectivity. Initially some patients questioned whether we really had to 'go virtual.' My archaic background almost seemed to dictate my second-guessing the decision. I had not realized just how much the office facilitated a transitional space (Winnicott, 1974), opportunity for patients to disclose long-shackled affect.

Such unexpected absurdities, together with the overburdening pressures of the quarantine—with the manic juggling of work and homeschooling and so on, as documented in innumerable op-ed columns—provoked a repetitive *situational* transference. Here as in younger days (and even as I recognized my situation as undoubtably privileged), I felt entrapped in a scenario akin to what Atwood (2015) calls the dilemma of the little psychotherapist, where the child's needs are sacrificed for those of the caregiver. In the scenario of COVID-19, the 'caregiver' is the pandemic itself. Its repetitively intrusive demands and implosion of boundaries are evocative of a circus-like home atmosphere I thought I had escaped.

As a child, I was beholden to the needs of alcoholic caregivers—also chaotic, intrusive, and epistemologically traumatizing (Brandchaft, 2010)—as I came to doubt my own perceptions and affectivity. As Winnicott (1971) states, in such scenarios the child becomes alienated from their own self-experiencing and ongoing embodiment.

The pandemic led to the repeated dread of such annihilations, as well as a heightened fear of clinical misjudgment during virtual visits, to make up for my 'taking away' the office, prompting extra pressure for me to stay on point, lest more patients decide that virtual treatment simply wasn't worth the trouble. I remain concerned even now that the grind of it all will tax me to distraction, also disappointing patients (to say nothing of loved ones), who are also fatigued and overwhelmed.

Yet this very situation, thrusting us all into the angst of uncertainty, became a bridge of sorts, a catastrophe in common, which patients each endured in their distinctive way. Drawing upon my own analogues of dread, overwhelm, and apprehension eventually illuminated—as the glowing filament of a bulb resists its current—what patients too felt but could not express (Atwood & Stolorow, 2016). In some cases, the 'trauma in common' also propelled a shared anger at political leaders of all leanings, wretched 'parents' who bungled the protection of their children/citizens.

With my patient Jan, what started as my sense of namelessly familiar suffocating responsibility, to 'manage' her subjective strife via my expertise, as she herself felt omnipotently responsible for others, eventually shifted to a deeper understanding: a hard won, shared achievement. Along the way, as I will illustrate, we diligently developed our connection, which she both craved and warded off.

For Jan too had been caught in the archaically strangulating expectation of caregiving her caregivers, a deeply instilled self-ideal now repeating with her anxious son, the bid to provide him with definitive reassurances, which she then reflexively asked of me—which I knew I could not provide even as I felt compelled to provide them: an echo of my own early demands to 'prop up' an entire relational system. Such imprisoning maneuvering, both co-transferentially (Orange, 1993) and as backgrounded by the pandemic, led to frustration initially, yet over time emerged from the fog as a more expansive horizon.

In the fatigue of COVID-19 (a term belonging to a dystopian future), I felt trapped in a familiar nightmare: the impossibility of providing emotional guarantees to an overwhelmed other, whom (I feared) could or would not tolerate the lack of definitive assurance, leading perhaps to abandonment of treatment (as with her previous therapists). As mentioned elsewhere (Haber, 2018), I grew up in a family wracked by depression, anxiety, and addiction; my younger sister fatally overdosed, lending an extra spark of urgency in some current cases. The pandemic made life difficult, but not impossible, though it sometimes seemed so.

Amplifying such complications was the Camusian absurdity of the pandemic, provoking what I call here an 'emotional quarantine,' or systemic demands to dissociate or disavow developmental strivings threatening to an inflexible system—re-provoked in my case as a 'hit' to my practice and loss of patients, with the frustrations of working remotely. The other shoe had dropped.

Such overburdening was existentially resonant, as I tried to mute my complaints (even in my own analysis!), for fear of being perceived as 'whiny' or over-privileged, failing to achieve the proper level of gratitude or recognition of underserved others (as with my caregivers, who trumpeted their woes while proclaiming our great fortune, especially compared to the poor).

The accompanying uncertainty—how long will it last, when will we have a vaccine? —then led to a foggy, extended Los Angeles 'June gloom' or thickening smoke from unseen yet encroaching flames (even literally, as California fires raged), all of the above befogging dyadic clarity, with fatigue and ongoing glitches; 'your connection is unstable,' indeed.

Camus argued for an enlivened response to absurdity, where finitude may be more than just deflating. We can nod to our precarious human position while remaining engaged in purposeful activity: a resistance to oppression while articulating the predicament that binds us.

His response inspires me to persist in empathic engagement, when dyadic process meets such challenges. This has included involuntary self-disclosure, as the in-person space is collapsed into the virtual, with cameras peering directly into our personal lives. My young daughter has made a few cameos, mostly to patients' amusement; occasionally I have forgotten to shave or wear a different shirt from the previous session. By patients' accounts this has humanized me, as we find humor and grief amidst our shared dystopia: siblings in the plague.

Surviving Lockdown and the Great Escape

When I was in fifth grade, my mother decided we should have a puppy. We bonded instantly and I took him everywhere. I also struggled on my own to toilet train him, somewhat haplessly, without assistance.

A few weeks later my mother abruptly decided we should not have a puppy. She was tired of dealing with 'everyone's shit,' as she put it, now including the dog's. One morning she ripped the bewildered creature from my grasp, and left to return him to the pound. I was inconsolable for hours. I can still recall the ache, the parental non-recognition of why I was upset, which after a while I myself began to question. My father was more attuned to his beer and baseball game, and as usual stayed out of it.

This unhappy anecdote shows something about the gross misattunement of noxious systems, in this case an alcoholic family marred by impulsivity, chaos, and indifference to children's needs. It also shows (speaking of absurdity) how an adopted puppy provided more affection and companionship than either of my caregivers, who were at the time locked in increasingly embittered impasse. This incident in fact—which repeated over the years, with two different dogs—happened at the time my father's brother died. My uncle had lived a sad, isolated life in his struggle with mental illness, and my father's drinking then took a dark, terrifying turn.

It was here that I took on even more caregiving responsibility, much as Brandchaft (2010) and Atwood (2015) describe, in not only the solo managing of my own emotional life, with adolescence approaching, but in looking after my siblings, per my parents' demands, as said parents were increasingly adrift and agitated about the lack of respect they felt they were due.

'It would do you kids good to suffer,' my father (a social worker) once dryly remarked.

What is so stingingly absurd about this narrative is that, after my own childhood loathing of my father's booze, his refusal to stop or talk to us about it honestly, I myself picked up the bottle in high school: an instant love affair I knew was dangerous but could not resist. I intuited it as likely disastrous, yet this 'puppy' would not be taken away.

One begins to see how early bedlam primes one for chaotic adulthood and a need for antidotal soothing. By my early twenties I was torn between the early ideal of responsibility and an insistence on having a 'good time' both liberating and destructive. Such divisive friction only drove the need for addictive soothing. It is remarkable how such subjective divisiveness paralleled the archaic relational divisiveness with photo-accuracy. I was in other words well trained for life as an addict (and later, an analyst). I had lived so long in affective lockdown, relieved initially by humor and play with my sister and brother, then drugs and alcohol in later years; thus, the contagion of addiction, all but ensuring a rigidly quarantined emotionality.

There are times when I again feel the remorse of lost opportunities. A possible job at 'Saturday Night Live' for instance, obtainable with more effort than I was willing to make (namely, a phone call). This was a show I grew up loving. I had a job lead, then hit a minor obstacle—and gave up immediately. There are many other such examples of blown leads, due I think to the fraught uncertainty arising with the most minor of risks, the strangulation of emotional development, even as I felt ashamed of being a 'quitter.' (A joint or two fixed it.)

Similarly for my patient Jeremy, the possibility of expansiveness was safer than any actual following through. Jeremy grew up caregiving his volatile, alcoholic mother, while longing for his distant, divorced father. He told me he found relief in imagining a solution to his dilemma of isolation and self-loathing, rather than following through—because as we discovered, it was too frightening to do so, as this risked disappointing himself or (worse) others. What struck me about this was its familiarity, no matter how deflating: an imagined expansiveness was close enough to 'real' in his experience, illusory hope less painful than none at all.

'Life is lived from the inside out,' a therapist once told me just before I stopped drinking. Previously, I imagined life's task was to find the 'perfect' circumstances and relationships into which to fit oneself—all but ensuring paralysis and distance from others, given their totemically significant approval. This is why mere 'interest' from potentially helpful others was dismissed, with no guarantee or immediate reward. Relationality was concretized or transactional in other words, with nary a sense of process or negotiation. What remain befogged was the anxious impossibility of differentiating from an inflexibly de-differentiating system.

One of the toxic legacies of addictive contexts is the way in which concretized or performative relatedness promises the preservation of connection, while ensuring ongoing distance. Neither is reliably fulfilled. The fraught attachment to abusers who are also protective is maintained via the child remaining symbolically tied as years progress, development remaining in the wings *ad infinitum*. When I left for college, my parents divorced almost immediately, having lost their 'counselor.' (I should have charged by the hour.)

I recall the look of panicked anger on my father's face whenever I dared bring up his drinking. It took the longest time in my own analysis to begin to acknowledge the impact of such silencing. Later, a formerly quarantined child turned adult might easily assume it is their own yearnings and foundational longings that remain criminally dangerous: a parallel to Camus' (1956) observation that the pain of a prisoner in endless solitary confinement can confirm over time, with unbearable anguish, the certainty of their guilt.

For those born into demanding surrounds, almost any possible expansiveness is shot through with risk, including of course analytically. Illusions or so-called fantasies, however paper-thin, remain safer than the void of a repeated abandonment never recognized archaically, that the patient may fear he or she cannot survive (Winnicott, 1974). In my practice I had to begin to view patients not as 'avoidant' but as unable to shake themselves loose of a prereflectively enslaving system. With Jeremy, I observed that his self-criticism flared after the merest whisper of a yearning or hope easily missed, his strivings quickly shuffled back into their cell, hidden along with the unrecognized strictures of his historical lockdown.

This may be why it is difficult for such patients to surrender the idea of some guaranteeing 'blueprint,' as Jeremy put it, or 'tools' that would ensure success (and stave off shame) in finding a spouse, promotion, and so on, to be found like produce in the grocery aisle. There remains such risk in even illuminating desire, likely to lead yet again to searing disappointment, vulnerability remaining disavowed, with the whispered hope of freedom. Best to have a solid plan if plotting a break from prison.

Easy as well to underestimate the protective power of illusion (i.e., an *imagined* expansiveness, or the denial of one's own compulsive drinking.) In my own case, prior to the pandemic, I somehow believed that the era of global disasters was over, that science could now guard us against something as medieval as a 'severe flu,' that nothing could upend the life I had worked so hard to achieve. I could not, in other words, imagine losing another puppy.

Yet it was more than just a rescue dog that was lost, in formative years. The losses of the pandemic reminded me, in its early days, of the many times my father announced he was giving up the bottle. One morning, when I was fifteen or so, he dramatically emptied his gin down the drain. He smiled proudly. Finally! Before long he was drunk again. I felt a disappointment that was painful because hope remained unseen, and now looked 'stupid.' I kept my mouth shut, of course, as the system rebalanced itself.

Such deflation can be a wrecking ball to a person's agency, as in the above examples of blown opportunities, whose deflation I already anticipated, soothed again by drinking, leading to another hangover and self-loathing, and subsequent need to drink again: this, in the end, felt like home.

***

Dyadic complications often ensue when I sense an unspoken demand to accommodate a patient's relational system, especially one rigidly focused on the literal (i.e., a blueprint), threatening to entrap me in suffocating binaries, with patients' hopes of a seamless or even telepathic understanding. Such pressures seep into the relational vocabulary or contextual 'forms of life' (Wittgenstein, 2009), a term for the lived language games or systems in place in any given context. In the clinical scenarios I discuss here, what predominated was the iron reinforcement of vulnerability's imprisonment, a taboo against the spoken emotionality I hoped to engage.

This can 'infect' my own analytic hopes with dread. When aversive processes take hold, I sometimes fear (as at the start of the quarantine) that my hopes of a co-created analytic emancipation for patients is a chimera, even a naïve one, that I am again bound to performative antidote or 'cure,' that even my cherished analytic freedom, along with my valued phenomenological inquiry, is insufficient in favor of the concrete. If I am the doctor after all, where is the prescription?

Most vexing of all for me is the tempting familiarity of this terrain, which I could navigate in the dark, written into my psychic DNA. It is easy to imagine cheering the patient up with a few slogans, suggest a workbook or two ('on them' if not completed), collect my fee and sign off, leaving both of us anesthetized. Hard to stay awake, in the fog of repetition. *Why are you killing me*, indeed.

Jan

Jan is an intelligent and attractive, successful businesswoman in her late forties, who sought my services several years ago after her son Ben, then a teenager, admitted he was addicted to Xanax. He went to an inpatient program and did well. After roughly two years of analysis, she stopped as Ben's life improved—returning a year later, after Ben again became addicted, this time to Percocet and Ambien.

Her older son Robert lives on the East Coast; he is much closer to his father (Jan's ex-husband), who lives close by. Jan resents their East Coast chumminess, overlooking Ben in favor of Robert's achievements in finance.

Ben lives alone in an apartment in San Diego. Jan worries about his roommates, who frequently like to 'party.'

Shortly before calling me, Jan found out Ben was freely prescribed Percocet for a skateboard injury to his back, with Ambien for insomnia. Jan is furious at the doctors, and at her son for omitting any mention of his Xanax addiction. Yet the venting of such terror and fury, she also fears, might provoke him to feel ashamed and/or hurt himself; he makes threats of self-harm from time to time, when he is furious or in the grip of craving, in the midst of his current detox, such threats withdrawn minutes later, to her exasperation.

Thus she tries to direct her wrath at Ben's doctors and the corruptions of Big Pharma, at Ben's indifferent father and brother, and most of all herself, for not paying more attention to his back injury and subsequent pain, as she dared to pursue her own interests, namely her business and time spent with a partner who has talked of proposing to her. (I sense vague disappointment with me, too, which she deflects.)

I am repeatedly, vividly reminded of her childhood abuse, a violent coercion into caring for caregivers, namely an alcoholic, self-pitying mother, and a raging narcissistic father. Her father beat her upon hearing complaints from her mother or delinquent older brother, for whom Jan was also responsible, even as he turned to pills, pot, and cutting himself, which led to severe punishment for *Jan*. Her own suffering has been unthinkable and impossible to express, leading to a long-term quarantine on authentic self-expression.

One of the difficulties here, as often with addiction and its frequent crises, is that the ongoing 'drama' of current relational fireworks vividly distracts from any historical associations. Adding to the challenge is that said history is literalized, wherein everything is as it appears, a hardened shellack deflecting reflectivity. In such totalitarian-like early systems, the family narrative is ever airbrushed to suit the powers that be, an example of epistemological trauma, often called 'gaslighting.' Incidents occur that require 'shouldering on,' end of story. Most patients remain terrified of any alteration of such a storyline.

To me it is plain as sunlight that Jan's dealings with her son are analogous to overseeing her brother in the archaic scenario, with her father's raging demands to 'fix him' embedded in unyielding self-ideals, a repeated terror of failing to deliver the impossible: the management of another's subjectivity entirely. To stray from her sentry duty, to not stay vigilant of others' needs is to risk another 'beating.' Trauma continues to collapse temporality (Stolorow, 2007), entrapping Jan—and, at times, her analyst—in an infinitely wearying, hopeless present, where empathic illumination is futile or impossible, all of this exacerbated by the pandemic's impositions. We both enjoyed meeting in person, our shared space now vanished in the fog.

In line with the brutal atmosphere, the micro-fascism of addictive demands, she ruminates over any potential pitfalls, having 'blown it' by taking time for herself to relax, not reminding her son to speak honestly to doctors. So wary she is of her own 'selfish' desires, that she tries to keep all traces of them at bay, her mind prototypically hijacked by the demands of the repeated, cult-like system. Meanwhile it is now the current addictive system, the compliance to compulsion, ruling as the de-facto leader; Jan is as enslaved to her son as he is to opiates and as she was to her caregiver system, perpetually held hostage by a terror impossible to name.

In fact, Jan began treatment, in a way not atypical, hoping I would help her cope with the stress of such enslavement, in not allowing it to be painful—i.e., to dissociate 'better,' secure a padlock lock on her quarantined affectivity, more vigilantly anticipate her son's needs, his own disavowed vulnerability. Opiates were tempting because of his own fears, that perhaps his injury would end his skateboarding, even as doctors assured him it would not.

With me Jan slowly realized, with traces of disappointment, that she could not reliably self-segregate in order to 'figure out' what was tearing at her (in fact, quite the opposite), stoking both her self-contempt and distrust of her own emotionality (as valued by her analyst, of whom she was sometimes wary). The surest 'fix' for her own rage, meanwhile, was Ben's safety, completely out of her control.

Now I am drawn into meandering discussions of what Ben might do to help himself, the pros and cons of this or that recovery or outpatient program, 'what are your thoughts on this, Darren?,' even as Ben rejects all suggestions, echoed in Jan's refusing my suggestion to attend Al-anon. Yet some of my guidance has been useful, as I helped find an addiction psychiatrist for Ben, whom he has not yet fired.

I occasionally sense that she sometimes wishes I could be Ben's father, or even hers, in a way that would directly relieve her of what she feels is impossible to tolerate, has never been shown how to tolerate: namely finitude and its vast Sisyphean uncertainties, themselves retraumatizing (Brothers, 2008). Jan remains hostage to systemic tumultuousness, as in childhood; I sense this better than I can communicate it to her, our language games under duress.

Ben calls her frequently or not at all, the latter even more unsettling to her. Meanwhile she pays his bills, schedules his psychiatrist and other appointments, driving down to San Diego to do laundry for him, since he's detoxing at home, under medical supervision. He seems to be making steady progress with occasional 'hiccups' in managing his own prescriptions.

What concerns me most is Jan's creeping depression, a sense of being smothered, with insomniac rumination over her mistakes, including marrying a lout, as 'I screwed up big time and my son is paying the price.' I cannot manage to bring in any transferential connections here, in terms of impossible self-ideals and where they might come from.

All of this of course echoes much of my own archaic experience, and only recently—prompted in part by the composing of this chapter—have I noticed, with no lack of astonishment, how familiarly provoking are these contexts of my *own* repetitive impulses, to assuage or 'fix' the problem, offer concrete suggestions to Jan. Her world is dangerous to me because it is easily re-assimilated, *familiar*.

I still stumble in moments where she poses 'yes or no' questions, the either/or, our habitual tap-dance of emotional detouring. I hear anxiety in her voice, as she realizes there is no definite answer to what she (or I) can do to quell uncertainty. I wonder if I disappoint her in not having such an answer, leaving her to face finitude alone, both of us handcuffed by absurd contingencies.

Such constriction is only exacerbated by COVID-19 isolation, as Ben sorely misses skateboarding (due to his injury) and his social life, and Jan misses dining out with her potential fiancé, after so many years of lonely evenings at home (pre-divorce), and we miss seeing each other in person. Her partner has been evasive of late; this infuriates and frightens her but serves in the end as another black mark against her. Surely she has driven him away with her 'whining' about her son.

My feelings for her are warm; I sense the brutalized vulnerability she is compelled to disavow, though it lurks in the shadows, a feigned hide-and-seek. She always displays grace under pressure, is witty, remarkably observant, and earnestly kind (to all but herself).

We speak at the end of the day, and both of our days are tiring, with Jan doing her best to help her son. Lately Ben has been more raw and explosive, possibly a sign that his taper is progressing, though his fury parallels (to my mind) the explosions of Jan's early caregivers. Sometimes she explodes back, followed by self-flagellation (for attacking a person suffering from mental illness); each appears to have precisely two 'moves' in their relational repertoire, attack and retreat. Jan's caregivers never allowed her to exist for herself, leading to the immediate undermining of her own need, leading to an unceasing push-pull (yes/no) that exhausts her and at times tuckers out her analyst.

One evening Jan informs me at the start that, per my earlier suggestion, she 'set a boundary' with Ben, in asking him not to yell at her. Is this a bid for my recognition? He responded by yelling, hanging up, then calling to apologize. He added, with (I intuited) a tint of vengeance, that he was having thoughts of self-harm: since he is obviously a total failure, life would be easier for everyone if he were gone. Usually this is followed by a manic apology. But not this time.

'So that's where boundaries got me,' she sighs, like an indictment, perhaps of both of us. She quickly adds, 'But he's diseased with addiction, who can blame him.' Here she blames *herself* for setting a boundary, breaking (to my mind) an archaic command fully camouflaged in present density.

She laments her outbursts at Ben and others, fears they have wounded her son, an unforgivable loss of control (a kind of emotional 'jailbreak'). She fights the urge to go to San Diego to check on him. She is angry his older brother is so self-involved. She asks if she should she should drive to Ben or not, or is this 'codependent,' *yes or no*; already I feel weary and eager for sleep.

She wonders if his allusion to suicide was prompted by the shame he felt when she asked him not to yell. I reiterate (silently noting that no such empathy is ever available for herself) that it was six in the morning when he called, that he has said such frightening things before. Yes, she says, but her anger does no one any good, as if wishing she could divorce *it*, too.

I wonder if she could possibly not answer the phone when dead asleep.

'But I'm all he's got!' she says, as if I have suggested hari-kari. She adds that Ben's psychiatrist has also suggested she do the same—but how can a mother abandon a diseased son? Before I can comment, she lurches into a monologue about how Ben might be 'blowing it' with this psychiatrist via demands for higher dosages, leading to said psychiatrist's irritation (and mine, quite honestly). Last week she snapped at Ben to 'shut up and listen to the doctor,' triggering his wrath and her anxious self-contempt ... she must get rid of this anger, as the question of whether to drive there lingers, yes or no, and what if Ben can never skateboard again *it's all he has,* why is her ex-husband such a prick, *though it was me who married him,* why won't Robert call his little brother, who does he think he is, *though shouldn't I be more happy for him* ... and does her staff think she's a flake ... And suddenly my daughter is knocking at the door, five minutes too soon. This morning I snapped at her, heard my father's wrath come out and was horrified ... as a kid I listened to his ramblings, over and over, the stink of gin and cigarettes, and here again is that foggy fatigue, bone deep and broad, I fear crashing into the rocks. Perhaps it's time for a quick reassurance: take two bumper-stickers and call me in the morning; I just want off this call.

But then a stillness ... this fatigue and overwhelm is what *Jan* must be feeling, *all the time,* as I recall a story she told me about her mother's rambling monologues, how as a child she suffered such rants, spoken dramatically to a rapt audience of one ... and here she is again, stuck in the status quo, an endless game whose mode is survival, as she all but firms up her own shameful failings and solitary confinement, inarguably convinced of her guilt.

I stop her, and ask what it's like for her when Ben yells at her or talks about overdosing.

She says something about how much he is suffering, since after all he's in pain, her snapping therefore 'unfair.'

'Eh, forget fair,' I say, and ask again. Then, after a long silence, I say, 'There's never any room for you, even in your own therapy.'

'Oh,' she says, as if surprised ... before adding, meekly, that maybe she's a bit tired of being everyone's slave. She then quietly describes how harrowing is the pile-on of Ben's threats to hurt himself, like being held hostage, it's outrageous given how hard she's trying, adding that 'if I'm so terrible he should just go ahead and put us *both* out of our misery!'

She then stops, as if shocked she could say such a thing. She weeps.

I remark how overwhelming it must be. She says, 'Yes, yes ... but he could die.'

'How terrifying,' I say.

'But what do I do? Go down there? Or is that unhealthy?' Our conversation stalls again in the yes/no. Either answer is 'wrong,' and the pressure is impossible.

Then I mention, somewhat drily, that now at least he is talking about pills, and not buying a gun as before, a scenario perhaps less horrifying...? A pause, before she laughs.

'Is that supposed to be progress?'

'Let's take it where we can,' I say. Now we are both laughing. I add that most people are not at their clearest in the wee hours of the a.m.

'Plus I need my beauty sleep,' she cracks. Then, with a groan, 'Jesus, how did I get into this?'

I sense a window as levity ebbs, remarking that she was *born* into this, never allowed to have her own life, hijacked by crazed caregivers; her son's current demands sound to me like echoes of her early life, where she was on the hook for her older brother, fearing any repercussions should she fail to do the impossible.

She hesitates, then says for the first time, 'Well there is an overlap there I suppose.'

I encourage her to continue, as she tentatively connects past and current terrors, the mitigation of which is again all on her shoulders. Enlivened, I underline the importance of her experience, her story, the telling of it to me, hoping we can keep it in the conversation, alongside her son's struggles. Terror of repeated agony is like a fog, I tell her. As it clears, our present options get clearer too.

She considers this, then murmurs her assent and a relieved, 'Thank you.'

In subsequent sessions, I support her sharing the way her son's anger wounds when he demeans her, even as she reflexively defends him. Perhaps both of them are suffering. She speaks to the anxiety of 'backing off,' allowing Ben to make his own decisions, that this lowers relational tension while provoking private terrors. Again, she can't win! After a few grueling weeks, as she tries not to watch the phone for any missed calls, he agrees to get an addiction therapist, freeing us up to talk about her hopes and existential alarm, past and present, along with an ever-enforced attunement to others, persuading her always that her own selfhood is toxic, necessitating affective quarantine.

'Every day growing up was a crisis, wasn't it,' I tell her, as she speaks of warring parents.

She responds, 'Yes, like trying to stay in the green zone. I never knew when the bombs would go off.'

'But no one ever noticed that part,' I say.

'Or cared,' she says.

I then speak of her dread and resilience, where at least her son now has a dedicated mother, when she herself had no one.

'Thank you,' she says again—almost mournfully, in a way never recognized by anyone.

Conclusion

This pandemic, like Camus' fictional plague and his other still-timely writing, reminds us of the fragility of our tranquilizing, everyday illusions (Stolorow, 2007). Easier at times to detach or sleepwalk, cling to our comforting veils, despite absurdity's inevitable unmasking. Such predicament becomes reflective of human embeddedness and fragility. Finitude in the end spares no one.

This is why I find it essential, in terms of understanding patients' experience, and my experience of patients, to carry on, grueling as the clinical hours can be, fighting for connectivity amidst tumult and fog. A world without empathic understanding is intolerable. Thus, the resistance to absurdity, encouraged by Camus (1942), in not succumbing to indifference or numbing, even as we encounter Sisyphean futility.

This is what happened with Jan, as her conscious persona had become nearly inseparable from archaic demands, now ritually enacted with her addicted son. Anxiety in such a scenario becomes a plague of its own. As a youngster Jan came to feel responsible for managing the world, as her traumatizing overburdening is again ignored and thus devalued of significance. (Insignificance becomes its own kind of trauma.) To take care of herself is abandoning, expressing her frustration to Ben is annihilating. Thus my perseverance to understand this conundrum, mitigate what has been archaically seared into self-imprisonment.

Sessions can be draining when solely virtual, as I sometimes pursue the elusive hope of 'proof' of my efficacy in the faces of patients, much as I looked for the smiles on caregivers' faces, secretly hoping I was enough. As with Jan, I was—provided I accommodated. Perhaps the seeds of such illusion (or hope, more charitably) of 'curing' the ailing of others were planted in such absent joy.

Yet it is once again the center of such dread, hopelessness, or overwhelm that provides an opportunity to assist in articulating that prohibited affect, pulsing with dark vitality. The impossibility of the patient's dilemmas is revealed, in ways they are asking themselves to expand while handcuffed to Brandchaftean ties. In joining them in the dilemma, we both sense what cannot be said: their unspeakable desire and Sisyphean despair. Thus, the analytic emancipation I hope to facilitate runs through and not around a shared distress, as the repeated detouring of such pain also challenges my own vulnerabilities.

Camus himself served as a little therapist to his deeply depressed mother, after his father perished in the First World War, when Camus was an infant. He self-quarantined for much of his adult life, due to a tuberculosis that should have killed him, even when he was coughing up blood and his doctors saw little hope.

In *The Plague* (1948), Camus warns against giving up in the face of existential uncertainty, insisting we fight and not surrender to the plague of anxiety or grim circumstance, for the sake of helping as many as possible.

Part of the tyranny of demanding systems is a crippling of personal meaning-making in favor of crushing conformity. What has helped sustain me, amidst the tumult described here, is the continued opportunity to make use of that experience in a way hopefully helpful to others.

I have attempted to illustrate in this chapter how the current catastrophe echoes earlier archaic scenarios, the crucial difference being that this time, in engaging relationally, there comes a chance to shift the paradox, from stark isolation to a *shared* absurdity: the asymmetrical loosening of dyadic strivings, while grieving their unacknowledged imprisonment. We are circumstantially bound to finitude, yet not completely handcuffed while we're here, even amidst foggy corona clouds, via the connectedness that keeps us alive. No bowing down, indeed.

References

Atwood, G.E. (2015). Credo and reflections. *Psychoanalytic Dialogues*, 25(2): 137–152.

Atwood, G.E. & Stolorow, R.D. (2016). Walking the tightrope of emotional dwelling. *Psychoanalytic Dialogues*, 26(1): 103–108.

Brandchaft, B. (2010). Systems of pathological accommodation in psychoanalysis. In B. Brandchaft, S. Doctors, & D. Sorter, *Toward an emancipatory psychoanalysis: Brandchaft's intersubjective vision* (pp. 193–220). New York: Routledge.

Brothers, D. (2008). *Toward a psychology of uncertainty: Trauma centered psychoanalysis.* New York: Analytic Press.

Camus, A. (1942). *The myth of Sisyphus* (J. O'Brien, trans.). New York: Knopf.

Camus, A. (1948). *The plague* (S. Gilbert, trans.). New York: Knopf.

Camus, A. (1956). *The fall* (J. O'Brien, trans.). New York: Knopf.

de Botton, A. (2020, March 19). Camus on the coronavirus [op-ed column]. Retrieved from www.nytimes.com/2020/03/19/opinion/sunday/coronavirus-camus-plague.html.

Haber, D. (2018). Yearning for Godot: Repetition and vulnerability in psychoanalysis. *Psychoanalysis, Self and Context*, 13(2): 132–148.

Lottman, H. (1997). *Albert Camus: A biography.* Corte Madera, CA: Gingko Press.

Orange, D.M. (1993). Countertransference, empathy, and the hermeneutical circle. *Progress in Self Psychology*, 9: 247–256.

Stolorow, R.D. (2007). *Trauma and human existence.* New York: Analytic Press.

Stolorow, R.D. & Atwood, G.E. (1984/2014). *Structures of subjectivity: Explorations in psychoanalytic phenomenology and contextualism.* New York: Routledge.

Winnicott, D.W. (1971). *Playing and reality.* Oxon, UK: Routledge.

Winnicott, D.W. (1974). Fear of breakdown. *International Review of Psycho-Analysis*, 1(1-2): 103–107.

Wittgenstein, L. (2009). *Philosophical investigations* (G. E. M. Anscombe, P. M. S. Hacker and J. Schulte, trans.). Oxford, UK: John Wiley & Sons.

Index